CHAMPIONS OF FREEDOM

The Ludwig von Mises Lecture Series

CHAMPIONS OF FREEDOM
Volume 37

Cars and Trucks,
Markets and Governments

Gary Wolfram, Editor

Hillsdale College Press
Hillsdale, Michigan 49242

Hillsdale College Press

CHAMPIONS OF FREEDOM
The Ludwig von Mises Lecture Series—Volume 37
Cars and Trucks, Markets and Governments

©2010 Hillsdale College Press, Hillsdale, Michigan 49242

First printing 2010

The views expressed in this volume are not necessarily the views of Hillsdale College.

Printed in the United States of America

Front cover: Steve Dininno; ©Images.com/Corbis

Library of Congress Control Number: 2009942801

ISBN 978-0-916308-30-8

Contents

Contributors

Peter Collier did his undergraduate and graduate work at the University of California, where he taught as a visiting writer. Mr. Collier previously served as an editor of *Ramparts Magazine*. The founder and former editor-in-chief of Encounter Books, he has also served as a State Department lecturer abroad in Scandinavia and Italy. His work has been nominated for the National Book Award and the National Magazine Award, and he is a Fellow of the National Endowment of the Arts. He has written for the *New York Times*, *Washington Post*, *Commentary*, *Weekly Standard*, *Vanity Fair*, and *The Wall Street Journal*, among others. He is the author of several books, including *Destructive Generation: Second Thoughts about the Sixties*, *Medal of Honor: Portraits of Valor Beyond the Call of Duty*, and (with David Horowitz) *The Fords: An American Epic*.

Myron Ebell is director of energy and global warming policy at the Competitive Enterprise Institute and chairs the Cooler Heads Coalition of nonprofit groups that question global warming alarmism. Mr. Ebell earned a bachelor's degree from Colorado College and a master's from the London School of Economics. He was a Regents' Fellow at the University of California, San Diego, and a member of Peterhouse at Cambridge University. Previously, he worked as policy director at Frontiers of Freedom; senior legislative assistant to Representative John Shadegg; Washington representative of the American Land Rights Association; and assistant to the chairman of the National Taxpayers Union. He has testified before numerous congressional committees, appeared frequently on television and radio, and his writings have appeared in a wide variety of publications.

John Engler is president and CEO of the National Association of Manufacturers. A former three-term Republican governor of Michigan (1991–2003), Mr. Engler is a graduate of Michigan State University with a degree in agricultural economics and earned a law degree from the Thomas M. Cooley Law School. Prior to becoming Michigan's 46th governor, he had served for two decades in the Michigan Legislature, including seven years as State Senate Majority Leader. When first elected in 1970, he was the youngest person ever elected to the Michigan State House of Representatives. In 1990, he became the first sitting legislator elected governor of Michigan in more than 100 years. He serves on the boards of Delta Airlines, Universal Forest Products, and the Wolf Trap Foundation, and is a past Chairman of the National Governors' Association.

Martin Fridson is CEO of Fridson Investment Advisors. Mr. Fridson received his B.A. cum laude in history from Harvard College and his M.B.A. from Harvard Business School. He has worked at Salomon Brothers, Morgan Stanley, and Merrill Lynch, and later formed FridsonVision, LLC, the first independent research company to focus on high yield strategy. He has been president of the Fixed Income Analysts Society, governor of the Association for Investment Management and Research, and director of the New York Society of Security Analysts. The Financial Management Association International named him Financial Executive of the Year, and he is the youngest person ever inducted into the Fixed Income Analysts Society Hall of Fame. He is the author of six books, including *Unwarranted Intrusions: The Case Against Government Intervention in the Marketplace.*

Paul J. Ingrassia is a Pulitzer Prize-winning journalist and author. Mr. Ingrassia has a bachelor's degree in journalism from the University of Illinois, and a master's degree in journalism from the University of Wisconsin. He began his career at the Lindsay-Schaub Newspapers in Decatur, Illinois, and then joined *The Wall Street Journal*. During his 31 years there, he served as the paper's bureau chief in Cleveland and Detroit, and later became president of the *Dow Jones Newswires* division. He writes on automotive issues for the *Journal's* op-ed page, the *Nihon Keizei Shimbun* of Japan, and other publications. He has appeared on NBC's *Meet the Press*, CNBC's *Squawk Box*, *The Newshour with Jim Lehrer*, and National Public Radio's *Diane Rehm Show*. Mr. Ingrassia is co-author (with Joseph B. White) of *Comeback: The Fall and Rise of the American Automobile Industry*. Most recently, he is the author of *Crash Course: The American Automobile Industry's Road from Glory to Disaster* (Random House, 2010). He is currently writing a book about specific automobiles that have helped shape modern American culture.

Joseph B. White is a Pulitzer Prize winner and senior editor in the Washington, DC, bureau of *The Wall Street Journal*, where he oversees coverage of a range of regulatory matters, including energy, transportation, and environmental issues. A graduate of Harvard University, Mr. White has worked for the *The Wall Street Journal* since 1987. For most of that time he covered the auto industry, serving as Detroit bureau chief from 1998 until 2007. He writes a weekly column, "Eyes on the Road," about the car business and the regulatory and social issues that surround it for the *Journal's* online and print editions. Mr. White is co-author (with Paul Ingrassia) of *Comeback: The Fall and Rise of the American Automobile Industry*.

Foreword

This is the 37th volume of Champions of Freedom, a book series that collects the papers delivered at Hillsdale College's annual Ludwig von Mises lectures. The essays in this volume, adapted from papers delivered in January 2009, focus on the American auto industry and the role of government in its decline and its possible revival.

The future of the auto industry today is uncertain—as was that of the industries it replaced 100 years ago. Change is the rule, not the exception, in modern economies. But the principles of free government, which place strict limits on government's power to regulate, remain the same as when our nation and our college were founded.

We present this volume at a time when the idea of limited government and the virtues of free markets are largely forgotten, and bureaucracy is on the rise. Hillsdale College is dedicated, in accordance with its old mission, to reversing these trends.

As Ronald Reagan said on our campus in 1978, "Freedom is never more than one generation away from extinction." It is our time now to stand in freedom's defense. I pledge that Hillsdale College will do its part.

LARRY P. ARNN
President
Hillsdale College
November 2009

Introduction

The CCA and Ludwig von Mises Lecture Series "Cars and Trucks, Markets and Governments," which took place January 25 to 29, 2009, and from which the papers in this volume are taken, was particularly timely, given that the auto industry was beginning a rapid transformation from a market industry to a fascist-socialist industry.

If we define the economic aspect of fascism as the private ownership of the means of production under government control[1] and socialism as government ownership of the means of production,[2] then the American auto industry has been transformed in a manner that lends itself to either definition. In any event, Friedrich Hayek, in his famous book *The Road to Serfdom*, made the point that socialism and fascism were basically two sides of the same coin, a centrally planned state,[3] wherein the principles and decisions of the central planner are substituted for that of individual consumers. This is a dangerous development for our economy and for our liberty.

Chrysler had already undergone a government bailout. In January of 1980, President Carter signed the Chrysler Loan Guarantee Act, which provided $1.5 billion in loan guarantees to help the company avoid bankruptcy. The government never took an ownership interest in Chrysler, and in 1983 the loans were fully paid back, leaving the government with a profit of $350 million. This episode was brought up in the recent policy debate as demonstrating that government intervention can be successful. Mises would acknowledge that it is possible for government to intervene in the market process with results that appear positive. He would add, however, that we cannot know that resources would not have been even more efficiently used had the government not guaranteed the Chrysler loans. After all, Chrysler's assets would not have disappeared. Rather they would have been taken over by another auto manufacturer, perhaps resulting in a more efficient auto industry that would have avoided the process that ended, some three decades later, with the bankruptcy of both Chrysler and General Motors.

The 2008–2009 auto industry crisis has led to much greater government intervention—both in terms of dollars and in terms of the depth of involvement—than the loan guarantees of 1980. The federal government began by directly loaning money to both Chrysler and General Motors, then began to dictate to the leadership of the corporations, and eventually took part ownership of the companies. Mises argued the point often that once you establish the principle that government should decide what is to be produced, or how it is to be produced, or that it should dictate individual behavior, there is no bright line to determine the boundaries of government action. Government intervention tends to lead to further government intervention, with government expanding its role over time until the economy transforms to a centrally planned state.[4]

Chrysler, GM, and Ford went before Congress in the fall of 2008 asking for money to sustain them through the coming months. When the Senate failed to pass legislation, Chrysler announced on December 17 that it would file for bankruptcy and shut down operations. On December 19, President Bush announced that money from the Troubled Asset Relief Program (TARP) would be used to loan $13.4 billion to General Motors and Chrysler, with another $4 billion to be loaned to GM in February. Ford Motor Company decided not to take the money, perhaps understanding—as Hillsdale College does—that government money leads to government control.

The Bush administration's decision to use taxpayer money that had been appropriated for the purpose of purchasing troubled assets from banks to lend directly to two of the three American auto manufacturers appears to violate the constitutional limitations on our federal government. The money was loaned despite, and indeed because of, the Senate's refusal to pass legislation to allow loans to the auto companies. It is interesting that Article I, Section 9 of the United

States Constitution states that "No money shall be drawn from the Treasury but in Consequence of appropriations made by law." Of course, that the TARP legislation made no mention of lending money to auto companies clearly suggests that this action was inconsistent with the Constitution.[5]

This lecture series took place at the point in time where the purpose of the taxpayer loans was, ostensibly, to prevent Chrysler and GM from entering bankruptcy. None of the authors had the benefit of knowing that both GM and Chrysler would soon end up in bankruptcy court.

On April 30, Chrysler filed for Chapter 11 bankruptcy and announced a deal with Italian carmaker Fiat. The U.S. government provided $6.6 billion in financing to cover the transition from the old Chrysler to the new Chrysler. As part of the June 1 bankruptcy agreement, the United Auto Workers Union's Voluntary Employee Benefit Association, which had been set up to fund retiree health benefits in the last labor agreement, gets 55 percent of the new Chrysler; Fiat gets 20 percent (with the opportunity to increase its share to 35 percent); the U.S. government gets eight percent; and the Canadian government gets two percent. On June 10, the agreement was finalized.

Despite the billions in loans and the warranty guarantees, General Motors followed Chrysler into bankruptcy court. The proposed settlement will be a section 363 sale of GM's assets to Vehicle Acquisition Holdings, which will be the only bidder. Vehicle Acquisition Holdings will be a consortium, with the U.S. government controlling more than 60 percent of the new company, the governments of Canada and Ontario twelve percent, the unions 17.5 percent, and unsecured creditors ten percent. The U.S. Treasury is providing $15 billion in debtor-in-possession financing for the deal. GM began negotiations to sell its Hummer brand to a Chinese company, Sichuan Tengzhong Heavy Industrial Machinery Company; its Saturn brand to Penske Automotive Group (which subsequently fell through); and Saab to Koenigsegg and other Norwegian investors (which has also failed to be completed).

One of the most important manufacturing industries in the United States is now firmly in government control. Whether one describes the ability of the Obama administration to remove the General Motors

CEO and the congressional mandate that the vehicle fleet average 35 miles per gallon as examples of fascism—or the government's 60 percent ownership of the new GM as indicative of socialism—matters little. In either case, a major sector of the American economy is now subject to the political process and the whims of government bureaucracy as opposed to individual choice and open markets. We will have reduced choice in the types of cars we drive and will be burdened by higher costs of production. Special interest groups from ethanol producers to unions will have added incentives to use the political process to benefit themselves at the expense of the consumer.

The essays in this volume give the reader a historical perspective on how we arrived at this situation and an enlightened discussion of the role of government in this industry. Former Michigan governor John Engler, while noting that the National Association of Manufacturers supported the loans from the TARP program, pointed out that his administration had been successful because it limited government and cut taxes. His thoughts are summed up in his admonition that it is better to cut or eliminate a government program than to drive away opportunity.

Myron Ebell offers an interesting look at the history of the automobile industry in the context of the freedom and mobility it afforded the average individual. His essay emphasizes the difference between market innovation and the stagnation of a centrally planned state. Paul Ingrassia presents an argument for the automobile as a sign of our culture, with examples such as the Model T, which provided mobility to the common man, and the innovative Corvair, the attack on which by Ralph Nader led to the product liability litigation revolution.

Peter Collier tells the story of the auto industry through the Ford family. His underlying theme is that continual innovation is the key to survival in a consumer-driven market economy. Joseph White discusses how the American auto industry went from world market dominance to bankruptcy in fifty years. His is a story of underestimating the competition, mismanagement of labor relations, and failure to innovate in a dynamic market.

Martin Fridson provides an informative discussion of the government's distortion of the ethanol market for motor fuel. He begins by pointing out that the first ethanol internal combustion engine was invented in 1826 and that Henry Ford's quadricycle was designed to run on ethanol fuel. Using public choice theory, Fridson demonstrates how a motor fuel that failed in the market place and offers little, if any, environmental benefit has managed to stay alive with enormous government subsidy.

The rapid socialization of the auto industry lends a certain timeliness to this CCA–Ludwig von Mises Lecture Series. The classical liberal insights of Mises—that the market process creates enormous efficiencies that cannot be matched by central planning—have been cast aside by the ruling elite of Washington. This, more than the policies themselves, poses a threat not just to the American auto industry, but to the economy as well. As Mises put it in his classic treatise, *Human Action,*

> This civilization was able to spring into existence because the peoples were dominated by ideas which were the application of the teachings of economics to the problems of economic policy. It will and must perish if the nations continue to pursue the course which they entered upon under the spell of doctrines rejecting economic thinking.[6]

We can hope that by next year's lectures the American public has turned against the socialization of our economy and returned to the classical liberal thought that Mises so clearly expounded in his long career.

GARY WOLFRAM
William Simon Professor of
Economics and Public Policy
Hillsdale College

Notes

1. See "Fascism," Sheldon Richman in *Library of Economics and Liberty*, at http://www.econlib.org/library/Enc/Fascism.html.
2. See George Reisman, *Capitalism* (Ottawa, IL: Jameson Books, 1996), p. 267.
3. Friedrich Hayek, *The Road to Serfdom* (Chicago: University of Chicago Press, 1944).

4. See, for example, Ludwig von Mises, *Economic Policy: Thoughts for Today and Tomorrow* (Chicago: Gateway Editions, 1979), Lecture 3.

5. Several other constitutional issues are raised by the whole process of government takeover of the auto industry. See, for example, Hans Bader, "Bush's Auto Bailout: Illegal or Unconstitutional," at http://www.openmarket.org/2008/12/15/administrations-unilateral-auto-bailout-illegal-or-unconstitutional/.

6. Ludwig von Mises, *Human Action*, 3rd rev. ed. (Washington, DC: Regnery), p. 10.

JOHN ENGLER

Michigan's Competitiveness
Yesterday and Today

In originally developing this essay, I worked with the concept and title "Michigan's Competitiveness, Yesterday and Today." With the many challenges facing the state and the nation, a broader choice was needed —"Michigan's Competitiveness, Yesterday, Today, and *Tomorrow*."

Even if President Obama and Congress could agree on an effective stimulus bill to rebuild confidence, shorten the recession, and spur job creation in 2009 (a big if—both the agreement and the effectiveness!) the United States, states like Michigan, and industries like the automobile industry face continuing, daunting challenges.

We need to talk about the path ahead and prepare to confront our new challenges. It is urgent that we build U.S. competitiveness for today and tomorrow. Only by ensuring our nation's economic competitiveness can we ensure jobs and prosperity for our citizens. We have all been made aware of the severity of the situation for manufacturing in Michigan and nationwide. The consequences can be seen in the data and felt in the pocketbook.

Sadly, Michigan continues to record the highest unemployment rate in the nation—10.6 percent in December 2008, 15.3 percent in September 2009. We know about the human toll. It extends much further than the Detroit automakers and their Tier 1 suppliers:

1

- Herman Miller, the office furniture manufacturer, cut 1,000 jobs in Western Michigan.
- Kalitta Air, a cargo transport airlines located in Ypsilanti, cut 200 jobs.
- International Paper in Howell cut 95 jobs. (They became the sixth Livingston County auto supplier to close in the last year.)

There have been many smaller layoffs, too. They all add up.

- Eaton, an auto parts manufacturer, laid off 31 employees in Marshall and 25 workers in Kalamazoo County.
- The McCormick Sawmill in Fountain let 13 workers go.

And not just manufacturers have been affected.

- Blue Cross Blue Shield of Michigan announced that as many as 1,000 people will lose their jobs, even as they ask for 55 percent rate hike on individual policyholders.
- AAA Michigan, the auto insurer, is laying off 146 employees.

Nationally, manufacturing production declined at an annual rate of 16.7 percent in the fourth quarter of 2008. This is the largest quarterly drop since 1980.

In 2008, an election year, the recession, plant closings, and layoffs brought a sharp decline in manufacturing production—7.7 percent. These are the largest four quarters of decline since the mid-1970s. U.S. factory job losses totaled 791,000 in 2008, with most occurring in the last half of the year, making it the worst year since 2001. Inevitably, retailers are being hit, too. In January 2009, Circuit City announced it would follow Linens 'n Things and Sharper Image into extinction.

We know the economy is in tough shape. But what do we do? What will be the impact on manufacturing and industries like the auto industry? What does this mean for Michigan…and for America?

Even those of us who stand on the side of markets acknowledge that the federal government has to respond. The decision to extend unemployment benefits was an easy call. Other decisions are more difficult. When President Ronald Reagan spoke at Hillside 31 years ago, he repeated a phrase he often used: "Even many of us who believe in free enterprise have fallen into the habit of saying when something goes wrong: 'There ought to be a law.' Sometimes I think there ought to be a law against saying 'there ought to be a law.'" That describes where we find ourselves today in Washington.

The National Association of Manufacturers (NAM) supported the federal loans and similar measures approved by Congress for the Detroit-based automakers.

The motor vehicle industry is the largest manufacturing industry in the U.S. Its contributions to the U.S. economy are critical, not just for the automakers themselves but for the hundreds of thousands of people employed by related suppliers and the auto supply chain. So the Detroit-based manufacturers are renegotiating, redesigning, and right-sizing in order to survive.

NAM also supported the economic stimulus legislation, but it favors a stimulus that does more than create short-term government jobs or that bases the distribution of a trillion dollars of government money on politics rather than efficacy.

We need to establish and fund priorities that improve our competitiveness in the global economy today *and* tomorrow. For one thing, that means expanding and upgrading our infrastructure. Historic investments in roads and bridges, airports, harbors, inland waterways and railroads, including transit systems, have not kept pace. The costs of too much congestion and too little capacity are choking our economy. It is time for a twenty-first century, satellite-based air traffic control system. We need to invest in our energy backbone—the transmission grid. We need to increase our supplies of electricity and further our goal of energy security. We need to increase the deployment of high-speed broadband connections: In addition to enhancing our security, this will help us meet urgent education and health care needs.

Competitiveness and long-term economic growth also require that we implement a tax structure that puts U.S.-based businesses in a better position to take on our global competitors.

You may be surprised to learn that the United States has the second highest corporate tax rate in the world: Only Japan's is higher. In country after country—large and small—our competitors have been cutting taxes. The list includes Germany, France, Sweden, and Mexico.

Government policies have a profound effect on economic growth and jobs. You can see it at the state level. Here in the Midwest, for example, Michigan's economy and jobs picture were in a rough shape before the recession hit in 2008. Sadly, that is not unprecedented. Neither my predecessor nor my successor as governor of Michigan have experienced even one month when the state's unemployment rate was below the national average.

In 1980, the year our last serious recession started, unemployment nationally averaged 7.1 percent. In Michigan that year unemployment topped 12 percent. In 1982, the year Congressman Jim Blanchard was elected govenor, the rate averaged 15.6 percent for the entire year. (It was 16.9 percent in November 1982.)

Fortunately, the 1990s were a very different story. President Reagan succeeded in delivering the right dosage of tax cuts and policy prescriptions. That initiated a period of economic strength that lasted until last year—especially if you overlook the tech collapse and the attacks of September 11, 2001. I took office as governor in 1991, and Michigan began to change its losing ways. We cut taxes, held the line on spending, and made it clear that the growth we wanted was growth in the private sector. Our reward was that Michigan enjoyed six years (1995 through 2000) with an unemployment rate lower than the national average. We celebrated the all-time record low unemployment rate in March 2000: 3.2 percent. It is hard to believe that was only nine years ago. We even restored the state's AAA bond rating, which had last been achieved three decades earlier.

Today, Michigan has again fallen behind. Some believe nothing could have prevented the pain so many of our families are experiencing. Others say it is just bad luck.

While macroeconomic trends and federal policies are beyond an individual state's realm of control, there are many things a state can do. Tax policies, labor policies, education and training policies all make a difference. States with similar underlying economies can experience very different results depending on the actions of a state's government.

About 200 miles down I-69 is the capital of Indiana. The economy and manufacturing sector of this neighboring state are very similar to Michigan's. In fact, its economy is even more dependent on manufacturing. Indiana Governor Mitch Daniels believes that government is "the last monopoly" that lacks accountability. He argues for measuring government programs and their effectiveness because "what gets measured gets done."

During Governor Daniels' first four years in office, the number of state employees was cut by 10 percent and a "pay for performance" system that rewards good workers was implemented. IBM was brought in to modernize and administer the state's inefficient welfare programs, saving Indiana some $1 billion. And he fixed the Department of Motor Vehicles: 96 percent of the public now says it is satisfied with the agency! A $600-million state budget deficit was turned into a $300-million surplus. The governor cut business taxes and, in 2008, achieved major property tax reform.

He advertised the state's improving business climate to manufacturers, and succeeded in attracting companies to move their headquarters there—domestic businesses like AT&T, Amazon.com, and Medco, and overseas firms like Nestle, Toyota, and Honda.

Obviously, the right policies matter. Of course, Indiana has felt the recession just like the rest of us. Faced with a budget deficit, Governor Daniels proposed spending cuts, no tax increases, keeping education as a priority, and not raiding reserves.

Minnesota Governor Tim Pawlenty admitted that the economic challenges we now face are "the worst we've seen in a long time." Nonetheless, he called for cutting the state business tax rate in half, from 9.8 percent to 4.8 percent over a six-year period.

North Carolina's Governor Beverly Perdue has ordered cuts in state agencies, a freeze on vacant jobs, and a halt to the millions of dollars spent on construction, purchases, and travel. She has authorized no tax increase.

My hope for Michigan is that the course Governor Granholm adopts is one that makes Michigan more attractive for investment, entrepreneurism, and the individual worker.

Businesses and manufacturers are constantly changing and adapting—doing everything they can to improve productivity, quality, and their ability to compete in the global marketplace. You often hear it said, "America doesn't make anything any more." This is wrong! Manufacturing in the United States produced more in 2007 than in any time in history, creating $1.6 trillion in wealth. To be sure, 2008 showed a drop, but we are getting better, more productive.

Is government keeping up? Is it becoming more productive?

I asked our NAM economist to analyze payrolls, percentage of GDP, and productivity over the last half-century for the manufacturing sector versus government. The results are striking. Over the past 50 years, from 1957 to 2007—

- Manufacturing employment fell 12 percent, from 15.8 million to 13.9 million. (Those are 2007 numbers: It is now below 13 million.)

- At the same time, manufacturing output increased 402 percent.

Fewer people making more things! Productivity is steadily increasing. And government?

- Employment in government—state, local and federal—has risen 187 percent from 7.7 million to 22.2 million.

- But government output has risen only 131 percent.

So per person, government productivity is actually falling!

The bottom line?

- Manufacturing—producing much, much more with fewer people

- Government—producing a little more, with a lot more people

True, government and manufacturing serve different purposes, but there is a lesson to be learned here. The competitive pressures of the marketplace lead to efficiency and productivity and, ultimately, economic growth.

A government that seeks to promote economic growth should support competition in the private sector and embrace it in the public sector. That is true at the federal level, and that is true for the states.

- Invest in infrastructure, in research and development, in education and training, the basics that allow manufacturers to innovate and improve and take on the competitors.

- It is better to cut or eliminate a government program than to drive away opportunity.
- Do not replace the wisdom of the marketplace with the priorities of the politicians. As the figures just cited suggest, the private sector is bound to do a better job.

Michigan has gone through hard times before, even worse times. In the 1980s, unemployment climbed so high, people put bumper stickers on their cars that read, "Will the last one out of Michigan please turn out the lights?"

Thankfully, Michiganians stuck around, continued to work hard, and made the difficult choices and necessary changes to steer us back in the right direction. It may be a slightly different course than had been charted before, but it is one that took the state forward.

I am confident that we—Michigan, the auto industry, and our nation—can right ourselves again economically. But we will succeed only if we compete instead of complain, and we choose growth over government.

JOSEPH B. WHITE

The Thirty Years War: How Detroit's Automakers Went from Kings of the Road to Road Kill

Let me begin by congratulating all of us. We are now in the auto business, the Sport of Kings, or in our case, presidents and members of Congress. Without your support—assuming you are fortunate enough to pay taxes—General Motors and Chrysler would very likely be getting measured by the undertakers of the bankruptcy courts.

But make no mistake. What has happened to GM is essentially bankruptcy by other means, and that is an extraordinary event in the political and economic history of our country.

In its early years General Motors survived the kind of management turbulence we have come to associate with particularly chaotic Internet startups. But with Alfred P. Sloan in charge, GM settled down to become the very model of the modern corporation. It navigated the Great Depression and negotiated the transitions from automaker to tank and military material producer during World War II, back to truck-and automaker. GM was global before global was cool, as its current chairman used to say. By the mid-1950s the company was the symbol of American industrial power—the largest industrial corporation in the world. GM held the distinction as the world's largest carmaker until just a year or so ago.

Can you believe that GM's biggest political problem was once the threat that the government might force it to break apart because it was *too* powerful? GM owned more than half the U.S. market. It set the trends in styling and technology; and even when it did not, it was such a fast and effective follower that it could easily keep Ford, Chrysler, or, heaven knows, American Motors in their places.

How does a juggernaut like this become the basket case we see before us today? You could write a book about this, but I will oversimplify and discuss five factors that contributed to the current crisis—a crisis that has been more than 30 years in the making.

1. Detroit has underestimated the competition—in more ways than one.

2. GM mismanaged its relationship with the United Auto Workers, and the UAW in turn did nothing to encourage GM (or Ford or Chrysler) to defuse the demographic timebomb that has now blown up their collective futures.

3. GM, Ford, and Chrysler handled failure better than success. When they made money, they tended to squander it on ill-conceived diversification schemes. When they were in trouble they often did their most innovative work: The first Chrysler minivan, the first Ford Taurus, and, more recently, the Chevy Volt are all ideas born out of crisis.

4. GM (and the other two) did indeed rely too heavily on a few gas-hungry truck and sport utility vehicle lines for their profits—plus the money they needed to cover losses on many of their car lines. They did this for good reason. When gas was cheap, big gas-guzzling trucks were exactly what their customers wanted—until they were not.

5. GM refused to accept that to survive it could not remain what it had been in the 1950s and 1960s—with its multiple brands and a dominant market share. Instead, it used short-term strategies such as zero percent financing to avoid having to reckon with the consequences of globalization and its own mistakes.

Let me put these points in a historical context.

Hindsight is 20/20, but as a nearsighted guy, I am not ashamed to make the most of the clarity that comes with time. In hindsight, it is apparent that the gas shocks of the 1970s hit Detroit at a time when the Big Three were particularly vulnerable. They were a decadent empire—Rome in the reign of Nero.

At the time, the pinnacle of Detroit auto art was the crudely engineered muscle car. The mainstream products were large, V-8 powered, rear-wheel drive sedans and station wagons. Detroit's marketing and engineering machinery did not comprehend the appeal of cars like the Volkswagen Beetle or the Datsun 240Z. I remember as a high school student being knocked out by a teacher's Toyota Celica, which, believe it or not, was a pretty cool car then.

But it took the spike in gas prices and the economic disruptions that caused—to really open the door for the Japanese carmakers. Remember, in those days Toyota and Honda were relative pipsqueaks. They had not much more going for them in the American market prior to the first Arab oil embargo than Chinese automakers have today or Korean automakers did 15 years ago.

The oil shocks, however, convinced a huge and influential cohort of American consumers—baby boomers—to give fuel-efficient Japanese cars a try. Equally important, the oil shocks persuaded some of America's most aggressive car dealers to give those Japanese imports a try.

The Detroit automakers initially dismissed reports about the high quality of Japanese cars. They believed that the Japanese automakers could be stopped by import quotas. They later assumed that the Japanese could never replicate their low cost manufacturing systems in America, initially believing that the low production cost of Japanese cars was the result of automation and unfair trading practices. (Undoubtedly, the cheap yen was a big help.)

Detroit's auto industry leaders decided that these small, economy cars would be marked as niche vehicles, and that the damage could be contained as customers grew out of the small-car phase of life.

They were wrong on all counts.

There were Cassandras—plenty of them. At GM, an executive named Alex Mair gave detailed presentations on how Japanese cars were superior to GM's—lighter, more fuel efficient, and less costly to build. He set up a war room at the GM Technical Center with displays showing how Honda had devised low-cost, high-quality engine parts, and how Japanese automakers designed factories that produced the same number of vehicles as a GM plant, but were roughly half the size.

Mair would hold up two connecting rods—the piece of metal in an engine that connects the piston to the crankshaft. One was made by GM. It was a bulky, crudely shaped thing with big tabs on the ends. Workers assembling engines would grind down those tabs so that the weight of the piston and rod assembly would be properly balanced. The other connecting rod was made by Honda. It was smaller, thinner, and more like a piece of sculpture than a piece of machinery. It didn't have ugly tabs on the end, because it had been designed to be properly balanced right out of the forge.

Alex Mair's point was simple: If you pay careful attention to designing an elegant, lightweight connecting rod, the engine will be lighter and quieter: The brakes will have less mass to stop, and the engine will feel more responsive because it has less weight to move.

Another person who had warned GM about the nature of the Japanese challenge was Jim Harbour. In the early 1980s, he tried to show GM executives just how much more efficient Japanese factories were by comparing the hours of labor per car produced. The productivity gap was startling: At that time, Japanese plants were twice as efficient as American plants.

GM's then-president responded by barring Jim Harbour from company property. Jim's son, Ron Harbour, still produces *The Harbour Report,* which examines manufacturing efficiency in the U.S. auto industry. Ron Harbour is now welcomed at GM and just about every other major automaker.

By the late 1980s, GM chairman Roger Smith had figured out that his company had something to learn from the Japanese. He just didn't know what. He poured billions of dollars into new heavily automated U.S. factories—including an effort to build an experimental "lights out" factory that had almost no hourly workers. He entered a joint venture with Toyota to reopen an old GM factory in California, the New United Motor Manufacturing Inc., or NUMMI. The idea was that GM managers could visit NUMMI and learn the "secret" of Toyota's assembly system.

Mr. Smith also launched what he promoted as an entirely new car company—Saturn. It was meant to pioneer both a more cooperative relationship with UAW workers and new ways of selling cars.

None of these were bad ideas. But GM took too long to learn the lessons from these experiments. The automation strategy fell on its face, because the robots didn't work properly, and the cars they built struck many consumers as blandly styled and poorly constructed.

NUMMI did indeed give GM managers valuable information about Toyota's manufacturing and management system, which a team of MIT researchers would later call "lean production." But too few of the GM managers who had gained that knowledge were able to make an impact on GM's core North American business.

Why was that? I believe it was because the UAW and GM's middle managers were focused, understandably, on the fact that Toyota's production system required fewer workers, only about half the number GM employed at a typical factory of the time. That was an equation the union would not accept. The UAW demanded that GM keep paying workers displaced by new technology or other shifts in production strategy, creating what became known as the Jobs Bank. That program discouraged GM from closing factories, and encouraged efforts to sustain production even when demand fell slack.

It is important to understand the relationship between GM's management and the UAW. If GM's leaders had listened to Walter Reuther in the 1950s and had used their power to demand that the United States adopt a single-payer, government-run health care system—instead of GM offering health insurance as a benefit in lieu of wages—today the UAW probably would not be a big issue and our government probably would not be in the awkward position of having to quasi-nationalize GM.

Likewise, if no Japanese or European manufacturers had built plants in the U.S.—in other words if imports were still really imported—the Detroit carmakers would probably not be in their current straits. Although it is likely consumers might be paying more for cars and have fewer choices.

"What if," however, is just another way of saying "So What?"

The fact is that the Detroit Three's post-World War II business strategies were doomed from that day in 1982 when the first Honda Accord rolled off a nonunion assembly line in Ohio. It soon became clear that Japanese automakers, and others, could build cars in the U.S. with relatively young, nonunion labor forces that quickly learned how to thrive in the efficient production systems those companies operated.

Being new has enormous advantages in a capital- and technology-intensive business like the auto industry. Honda, Toyota, Nissan, and later BMW, Mercedes, and Hyundai had new factories, often subsidized by the host state, that were designed to use the latest manufacturing processes and technology. They had new work forces, which was an advantage—but not because the workers were paid less per hour. Generally nonunion autoworkers earn roughly the same as UAW men and women earn in GM assembly plants. The advantage the new nonunion companies have is that they do not pay for the health care and pensions of hundreds of thousands of retirees.

Moreover, these new American manufacturers did not have to compensate workers for accepting the change from the old mass production methods to the new lean production approach. GM did, which is why it created the Jobs Bank. It hoped that if UAW workers believed they would not be fired as GM grew more efficient, they might embrace the new methods.

Of course, we know how that turned out. The Jobs Bank became little more than a welfare system for people who had nothing more to contribute to the company because GM's dropping market share had made their jobs superfluous.

Health care is a similar story. GM's leaders—and the UAW's—knew by the early 1990s that the combination of rising health care costs and the longevity of GM's retired workers threatened the company. But GM management backed away from a confrontation with the UAW over health care in 1993, and in every national contract cycle after until 2005 when it finally became clear to everyone that the company was near collapse.

In testimony before Congress in December 2008, CEO Rick Wagoner said that GM had spent $103 billon during the preceding 15 years to fund its pension and retiree health-care obligations. Averaged over those 15 years, the per-year cost was nearly $7 billion—more than GM's capital spending budget for new models this year.

Why wasn't Rick Wagoner making this point in 1998, or 1999, or even 2003?

Even now, GM doesn't seem willing to treat the situation like the emergency it is. Under the current contract, the UAW will pay for retiree health-care costs with a fund negotiated in last year's contract, but that won't start until 2010. GM is on the hook to contribute $20 billion to the fund over the next several years, unless it can renegotiate that deal under federal supervision.

As Rick Wagoner told the House Financial Services Committee: "And obviously, if we had the $103 billion and could use it for other things, it would enable us to be even further ahead on technology or newer equipment in our plants, or whatever."

Whatever, indeed. This is a good place to talk about the mistake that Detroit made that matters the most to most people: Quality. By quality, I mean both the absence of defects, or "things gone wrong," and the appeal of the materials, design, and workmanship built into a car. I believe that most car buyers equate a vehicle's durability and reliability over time with "quality."

The failure in the 1980s of the Detroit automakers to keep pace with the new standards of reliability and defect-free assembly set by Toyota and Honda is well known —and it haunts them still. The really bad Detroit cars of the late 1970s and early- to mid-1980s launched a cycle that has proven disastrous for all three auto companies. Poor design and bad reliability records led to customer dissatisfaction, which led to weaker demand for both new and used American cars. Customers were willing to buy Detroit's brands—but only if they received a discount in advance for the mechanical problems they assumed they would have.

From the 1990s to now, the surveys that industry executives accept as reliable began to show that the best GM and Ford new models were just as good as—and in some cases better than—comparable Toyotas or Hondas or Nissans in terms of being defect-free.

But Detroit still had a problem. Mainly because of labor and legacy costs, with a big helping of inefficient management thrown in, Detroit was starting out with per-car costs at least $2,000 more than the best Japanese brands. To lessen that built-in disadvantage, GM and Ford (and Chrysler) resorted to aggressive cost-cutting and low-bid purchasing strategies with their materials suppliers.

Unfortunately, customers could see the "low bid" approach in the design and materials the automakers used. Even though objective measures of defects and "things gone wrong" were showing that the new Detroit cars were getting better and better, customers still demanded deep discounts for new and used Detroit models, compared to Toyota and Honda (and in the luxury market, BMW, Lexus, and Mercedes). Customers drove down the resale values of used cars, which made it harder for Detroit to charge enough for the new vehicles to overcome the cost gap.

GM, Ford, and Chrysler compounded this problem by trying to generate the cash to cover their health care and pension bills by building more cars than the market demanded, and then "selling" them—"selling" here needs to be in air quotes—to rental car fleets. When those fleet cars bounced back to used car lots, and into competition with new vehicles that were essentially indistinguishable except for a higher price tag, they helped drive down resale values even more.

The billions and billions spent on legacy costs are matched by billions more in revenue that the Detroit carmakers never saw because of the way they mismanaged supply and demand. This is why the American brands appear to be lagging behind not just in hybrids—where the durability of that market remains to be seen—but also in terms of the refinement and technology offered in their conventional cars.

Detroit has been on a cycle of hubris–fall–repentance–Phoenix-like recovery–hubris pretty much every ten years since the government bailed out Chrysler in 1980.

The spectacle of the diminished former Big Three CEOs and the UAW president groveling before Congress has us focused on how Detroit has mishandled adversity. A more important question is, Why did they do so poorly when times were good?

Consider GM. In 2000, Rick Wagoner, his senior executive team, and a flock of auto journalists jetted off to a villa in Italy for a seminar that would examine how the GM of the twenty-first century was going to look. Mr. Wagoner and his team talked a lot about how GM was going to gain sales and profit from a "network" of alliances with automakers such as Subaru, Suzuki, Isuzu, and Fiat. They talked about how they were going to use the Internet to turbocharge the company's performance, and so on.

Five years later, all of this was in tatters. Much of the capital GM had invested in its alliance partners was lost when the company was forced to sell out at distressed prices. Fiat was the worst. GM had to pay Fiat $2 billion to get out of that deal, never mind the $2 billion it had spent up front to buy 20 percent of the company. GM said it saved $1 billion a year thanks to the Fiat partnership. Whatever those gains were, they obviously did not help GM become profitable.

At least GM didn't use the cash it had collected during the 1990s' boom to buy junkyards as Ford had. But GM did sense a money-making opportunity in selling mortgages, and so plunged its GMAC financing operation aggressively into that market. GM didn't see the crash in subprime mortgages coming either, and now GMAC is effectively bankrupt and being restructured with government assistance.

Its many critics argue that what GM should have done with the money they spent on UAW legacy costs and bad diversification plays was to develop electric cars and hybrids, and not to continue to base their U.S. business on the same large V-8 powered, rear-wheel drive formula they had used in the 1960s, although now these vehicles were packaged as SUVs, not muscle cars.

Detroit did depend too heavily on pickup trucks and SUVs for profits, but they did so for understandable reasons: These were the vehicles that consumers wanted to buy. And—although this isn't what anyone administering the CAFE standards would say—these were the vehicles that government policy encouraged them to build.

GM made profits of as much as $8,000 each on those vehicles, while it lost money on its cars. Federal fuel economy rules introduced in 1975 forced GM to shrink its cars so that they could average 27.5 miles per gallon. GM did this poorly. Anyone who remembers the Chevy Citation or the Cadillac Cimarron knows what I mean.

But federal laws allowed "light trucks" to meet a lower mileage standard. This kink in the law allowed GM, Ford, and Chrysler to design innovative products that Americans clamored to buy when gas was cheap—the sport utility vehicle. When Ford launched the Explorer, and GM later launched the Tahoe and the upgraded Suburban, the Japanese companies were envious, especially Toyota. Toyota worked its way toward its first annual loss in 70 years (this occurred in 2008) by building too many factories in the U.S. in order to build more SUVs and pickups.

One irony of the current situation is that the only vehicles likely to generate the kind of cash GM and the others need right now are those same gas guzzlers that Washington no longer wants them to build.

Even Tom Friedman has come to realize that you can't ask Detroit to sell tiny, expensive hybrids when gasoline is under $2 a gallon. We have two contradictory energy policies. The first is that we need cheap gas at all costs. The second is that Detroit should substantially increase the average mileage of its cars to 35 or even 40 miles per gallon across the board. How the Obama administration will square this circle, I don't know, but I would note that Mr. Obama's energy secretary, Steven Chu, recanted his support for higher gas taxes during his confirmation hearings.

So where are we now? GM has become Government Motors. With the U.S. Treasury standing in for the DuPonts of old, GM is going to try to reinvent itself—as it did in its early years after Alfred P. Sloan and the DuPonts took the company away from Billy Durant.

One challenge for GM—among the many in this process—will be coming to terms with the reality that the U.S. market is too fractured and has too many volume manufacturers for any one of them to expect to control the kind of market share and pricing power GM had in its heyday.

There are now ten foreign-owned automakers with factories in the U.S. According to Wardsauto.com, these automakers assembled 3.9 million cars, pickups, and SUVs in 2007, before demand began to collapse. That is more than the combined U.S. production of Ford and Chrysler.

GM's efforts to cling to its 1950s self—with the old Sloanian ladder brands of Chevy, Pontiac, Buick, Cadillac *plus* Saturn, Saab, Hummer, and GMC—have led the management into one dark wood of error after another. Since 2001, GM's marketing strategy has dwindled to a single idea: Zero Percent Financing.

Zero percent financing was the automotive version of the easy credit that ultimately destroyed the housing market. Cut-rate loans, offered to decreasingly credit-worthy buyers, propped up sales and delayed the day of reckoning. But it didn't delay it long enough. The house of cards began tumbling in 2005. I would say it has now collapsed fully.

Between 1955 and 2007, GM managed to earn a cumulative total of $13.5 billion. That is three-tenths of one percent on the total revenues during that period, which were more than 4 trillion—and those are nominal dollars, not adjusted for inflation. Between 1990 and 2007, GM lost a combined total of about $33 billion.

Old habits die hard. Within hours of clinching a $6 billion government bailout, GMAC and GM were back to promoting zero interest loans.

During the 1980s and 1990s, GM leaders refused (and I believe some continue to refuse) to accept that the presence of so many new automakers in the U.S. market—more than at any time since the 1920s—would mean that the company's U.S. market share going forward would not be returning to the 40 percent of the mid-1980s, or the 30 percent levels of the 1990s, or even the mid-20 percent range we have seen more recently.

One thing to watch as GM tries to restructure will be the assumptions the company makes about its share of the U.S. market going forward. If they call for anything higher than 15 percent, I would be suspicious.

Since we all are now part owners of this enterprise, we need to pay close attention. What is about to unfold has no clear precedent in our nation's economic history. The closest parallels I can see are Renault in France, Volkswagen in Germany, and the various state-controlled Chinese automakers. But not one of these companies is as large as GM, and not one offers a model of what GM should want to become.

As I have tried to suggest, it is hard enough for professional managers and technicians, people with a clear profit motive, to run an enterprise as complex as a global car company. What will be the fate of a quasi-nationalized enterprise with managers whose "board of directors" will now include 535 members of Congress plus various agencies of the Executive branch? As a property owner in suburban Detroit, I can only hope for the best.

PETER COLLIER

The Fords

This is the winter of the auto industry's discontent, a time filled with grim auguries of bankruptcy, job loss, executives at sea in their own ocean, and bailouts that, hopefully, will work—but that cannot help but make one think of that famous bridge to nowhere.

It is always possible that what we are seeing take place is something more subtle and more positive: The creative destruction that is the genius of capitalism, that invisible process by which new industrial arrangements arise from of the old. Perhaps.

But right now it feels more like an ending than a beginning. So it is worth taking a little time to recall the epic narrative that the one-hundred year rise of the auto industry has been and how significant a role it has played in our national life. The best way to do this is by focusing on the Ford Motor Company, whose story is, by far, the most interesting chapter.

In its scope and sheer human drama, the Ford story is unique in the auto industrial age. It has elements of Greek tragedy, where men dare the gods and pay the price for their hubris, and elements of Shakespeare's history plays, where immoral acts continue to infect the social structures in which they have been committed until a cleansing occurs. But this story also reinforces an important lesson: In the final analysis history is made by individuals, not by impersonal "scientific" forces, as those we defeated in the Cold War used to like to say.

The story properly begins on June 4, 1896, when Henry Ford, 33 and already considered a failure, finally completed a project he had been working on for months every night after finishing his day job as a Detroit machinist. It was a quadricycle with a gasoline engine. The bar seat was big enough for two, the horn was a doorbell and the steering mechanism was a tiller. In a warning sign of the blindness that coexisted uneasily with his visionary streak, Ford hadn't realized that his "baby carriage," as he lovingly called it, small though it was, was too big to fit through the doorway of his workroom. But he wouldn't be stopped by that. Grabbing a maul, he knocked a hole in the brick wall and, with a friend on a bicycle riding ahead to warn people walking on the streets, he drove off, it is tempting to say, into history.

Ford endured years of fits and starts after his first vehicle emerged from that knocked-down wall. Others got ahead of him in the infant auto business as he acquired backers and discarded them when they wanted to exercise control. But in 1903, seven years after that first ride, he finally found the right chemistry and set up the Ford Motor Company.

At this point most Americans had heard of the automobile, but few had seen one. Autos were not that unusual a sight in Detroit, which had become the center of the experimentation required to give an industry critical mass—the automotive equivalent, say, of Silicon Valley three decades ago. Among the other auto entrepreneurs was a man named William Durant, who had taken over a tiny company obscurely named Buick and positioned it as the first step toward the organization he envisioned as General Motors.

Unlike his early competitors, Henry Ford didn't just want to build cars, he wanted to build *the* car. He believed he had achieved his dream in 1909 when his company brought out the Model T. It had 4 cylinders and 20 horsepower and went 50 miles per hour with no problem. He spoke of it in almost biblical terms, calling it "an automobile for the multitude."

In 1910, the first year of full production, 19,000 Model T's were sold. Two years later 80,000 were sold. It was a cultural sensation. That first car did what automobiles would continue to do better than any other device ever created: It captured the American imagination. The

Model T immediately entered folklore as the beloved "Flivver" and "Tin Lizzie." In many homes, it was treated like a household pet. It became America's car in the same way that the Yankees would become America's team.

And it soon made Henry Ford the richest man in the world.

Two things in addition to the Model T put Ford on the map. The first was the assembly line, an idea that Henry didn't come up with himself but that he developed better than anyone else. In 1913, it took 12 man-hours to construct a Model T, a year later, when the assembly line was fully operational, one could be built in about 90 minutes.

Henry Ford's other Big Idea was the decision to raise the daily wage of his employees from $2.50 to $5. It gave him a reputation as a humanitarian, which was then well deserved, for at this stage of his life he believed deeply in the dignity of labor. But the $5 wage was also a shrewd financial move. Absenteeism went from 10 percent to under 1 percent a day. And he created a huge new consumer base for his own products because the men who made Fords could now afford to buy them.

Within a few short years, Henry Ford had become an American icon. His importance in the national imagination was symbolized by the mammoth plant he began to build on the Rouge River: Its floor space added up to over 200 acres and it took 5,000 janitors to clean it every night. Ford was different from John D. Rockefeller and the other robber barons of the preceding generation. He had not built this empire by running others out of business or squeezing them until they had no choice but to sell out to him. Ford built his business through innovation and an unflinching determination that at times amounted to tunnel vision. The country mythologized him almost overnight as a rugged individualist whose practical, cracker-barrel insights could be transferred from the auto industry to other areas of life. With so many listening, Henry Ford concluded that he must actually have something to say. He began to offer what he regarded as commonsense solutions to the problems afflicting every aspect of national life. Throughout the 1920s, he was routinely singled out by his countrymen as the man they would most like to have as president.

But in the 1920s, at the peak of his prominence, another side of this odd man appeared. He became embittered when populism, which was at the core of his worldview and which he had hoped to make dominant in America, collided with what he saw as more entrenched forms of social and financial power. He could not keep America out of World War I, for instance, or prevent it from succumbing to the immoral excesses of the Jazz Age. He began to look suspiciously at the modern world developing with dizzying velocity all around him, a world he didn't seem to realize that he, more than anyone else, had created by allowing Americans to uproot themselves from their rural past and motor down the road to their urban future. Wherever he looked, Ford saw social dislocation and random and threatening newness.

Turning inward, he became contemptuous of experts and expert opinion about the meaning of things, bitterly uttering his famous comment, "History is bunk." He looked for occult explanations for things that were beyond his control. Like others pursuing this question, he found an easy answer: the Jews.

Ford bought a little paper called the *Dearborn Independent* and, in a sign of what had come over him, turned it into the nation's most vitriolic organ of anti-Semitism. He disseminated as truth *The Protocols of the Elders of Zion*, a forgery created decades earlier by the Czar's secret police, which purported to be the Jews' secret plan to control the world. He published a vicious book titled *The International Jew*, which didn't do all that well in the United States, but had avid readers in Europe. One of them was Adolph Hitler, who, during his rise to power, kept a photo of Henry Ford on his desk.

The gradual fermentation of the Great American Optimist into the Great American Crank took place outside the field of vision of most Americans. But the effects of this transformation were felt daily by the company Ford had created and by his son Edsel, whom he envisioned as its future leader.

Edsel Ford had grown up cocooned in his father's fame, never doubting for a minute Henry's greatness or the responsibility he himself had to extend its impact. He had willingly given up going to college to stay at his father's side. In 1919, at the age of 25, he was rewarded with the presidency of the Ford Motor Company and millions of dollars in stock, which Henry alone controlled, having methodically bought off his early investors.

Slim, quiet, artistic in temperament, Edsel was sometimes photographed in a blazer and white flannels, with a faraway Gatsby-esque look in his eyes. A member in good standing of the modern world Henry was coming to despise, he and his wife Eleanor had an estate at Gaukler Pointe that became a meeting place for second-generation members of the "gasoline aristocracy," and who were bringing modern art and music to Detroit. Edsel had three sons—Henry II, Benson, and Bill—and his only dream for them was that they inherit the great company he was trying to make a rational place in both human and industrial terms.

By the mid-1920s that company, despite the iconic status of the Model T, was in trouble. Edsel begged his father to see what was happening at GM, which had overtaken Ford in sales for the first time in 1924. Alfred Sloan, who had followed William Durant as president and who made GM into a giant corporation, had introduced such innovations as hydraulic brakes and self-starters. When Edsel tried to implement these innovations as well, Henry said no. Sloan's designers at GM were creating cars based on a new premise: that the automobile was breaking out from the workaday utilitarian world into a dreamscape where the growing middle class could objectify its hopes and ambitions and hunger for status. When Edsel pushed for new styles, Henry said no. When GM began to sell cars on credit, Henry said no.

GM saw the auto marketplace in its growing complexity as having many consumer "stalls," or product niches. It understood that because cars were becoming status symbols, buyers would not be content to stay within one stall over their lifetime. Rather, consumers would seek to move upward from one brand to another as they became more affluent—going from a Chevy to a Pontiac to a Buick or an Olds and perhaps on to a Cadillac in a single driving lifetime. At Ford there was only one stall—the one occupied by the Model T, the once and future car. Henry Ford wanted to know what was wrong with that. He kept repeating the ingenious advertising slogan he had come up with years earlier: "It gets you there and it gets you back."

Working outside his father's view, Edsel assembled a team that designed two classic autos—the Lincoln Zephyr, a mid-sized Art Deco classic, and the Lincoln Continental, a homage to the great European touring cars of the era. Henry scorned them both and made sure they remained in the shadows of the company.

Finally, in 1927, in the hope of arresting the company's slide, Henry allowed Edsel to convince him to discontinue the Model T in favor of a sharp new design—the equally classic Model A. Because of pent-up demand on the part of Ford loyalists, dealerships erupted into mob scenes when it appeared. Close to one million Model A's were sold its first year. Henry thought that this would do it and that time would again stand still. But in 1928, GM brought out a new 6-cylinder Chevy that challenged the Model A for the top spot. Then Walter Chrysler's new company entered the race with its dashing Plymouth.

By 1931 GM held 31 percent of the market and Ford had 28 percent. The following year, in 1932, Edsel tried to pull even again by bringing out the V8. It too was an immediate sensation, but it was Ford's last new model until after World War II. By 1936, GM had 43 percent of the market, followed by Chrysler with 25 percent. Ford trailed with 22 percent. Edsel managed to get the Mercury division into operation, but it was too little, too late.

GM's greatest asset was not just the variety of its cars, but its organizational structure. It had become the model of the modern corporation, decentralized so that product lines were semi-independent units working in a competitive but coordinated way for the greater good of the larger enterprise. It created a situation that would allow the most innovative and talented executives to rise to the upper reaches of the flowchart.

The Ford Motor Company, by contrast, remained a feudal institution, with a Mad King and a Doomed Prince. All that was needed to make the drama complete was a Usurper. And by the early 1930s, it had that too, in the person of a notorious Detroit character named Harry Bennett.

Harry Bennett was a former boxer and Navy diver who worked for Ford as a watchman. Henry happened to meet him during one of his random tours of the plant, as he was looking for decisions by Edsel he could reverse. He was smitten by Bennett, a tough guy who was on a first-name basis with members of the Detroit underworld. Ford began to use Bennett as a sounding board for his increasingly paranoid ideas about the way the world worked. A savvy listener, Bennett knew how to encourage Henry in his dark views. With labor problems on the horizon, Henry put him in charge of security at Ford. This gave Bennett the keys to the kingdom.

Edsel saw unionization as inevitable, as did Chrysler and GM. But Henry felt betrayed by the workers to whom he had been so generous back in the day. He ordered the assembly line sped up, leading to the dehumanizing frenzy famously satirized by Charlie Chaplin in the classic film *Modern Times*. He allowed Bennett and his gang of goons to range freely through the plant, beating up union sympathizers and creating a system of informants. This reign of terror culminated in the famous Battle of the Overpass when CIO organizer and future president Walter Reuther was attacked and badly beaten. When his bloody photograph appeared the next day on front pages all over the country, the American public saw it as the face of the workingman at Ford.

The company lost the unionization battle, but Bennett continued to insinuate himself into Henry's increasingly disordered worldview as the good son, willing to do what was necessary, while Edsel was increasingly marginalized as the weak son, too riddled with qualms and compunctions, in the old man's view, to be entrusted with the company.

With the coming of war, Edsel worked hard to convince his father, a natural isolationist, to allow the Ford Motor Company to become part of the Arsenal of Democracy. The old man finally allowed a great aircraft plant to be built on farmland he owned in Willow Run. Applying the techniques of auto manufacturing to airplanes, Willow Run was turning out 540 B-24s a month by the end of the war. But Edsel didn't see this triumph: He died of stomach cancer in 1943. His father, now 80 and more unstable than ever after suffering a stroke, reassumed the presidency of Ford with Harry Bennett behind him, pulling the strings.

There had been 200 car manufacturers in 1920, 3 in 1930, and 17 in 1940. It wasn't clear that Ford, a crippled giant, would make it into the postwar world. But the miracle at Willow Run had shown how vital a part of the national economy the company was. For a time there was talk in Washington of nationalization. Instead, it was decided to give Edsel's eldest son, Henry II, a 24-year-old Navy officer, an early discharge so that he could come home and try to take hold.

All three of Edsel's sons had grown up embedded in the auto industry. Priceless home movies at the Ford Archives show them racing around the family estate in one-of-a-kind miniature Model A's built especially for them. It wasn't clear that Henry II, elevated by the rules of primogeniture, was the best equipped of the three for the task ahead. He looked pampered and somewhat soft, and it was easy not to take him seriously. He had made a name for himself in college as an unrepentant plagiarist of term papers, a committed anti-intellectual, and a Good Time Charlie.

Yet in one respect Henry II was very well prepared. Like his brothers and his sister, he had grown up watching his grandfather's brutal assault on his father and he was gunning for revenge. Asked by a family friend why he had come home to take on what seemed an impossible task, Henry II said, "Because my grandfather killed my father and turned my father's company over to a thug."

Egged on by Bennett, the elder Ford locked Henry II out of the office he had tried to occupy at the plant. Henry II found another office and gathered a small team to back him, chief among them was a tough-as-nails former FBI man named John Bugas. The younger Ford created a parallel executive universe and did in fact manage to overturn his grandfather's capricious postwar decision to scrap the Mercury and Lincoln divisions.

But Bennett was always in the way. He had gotten Henry to appoint him executive vice president and a board member. At one point in 1945, Henry II felt so stalemated that he told his mother that he would probably fail in his quest. Eleanor Ford went to her father-in-law and told him that she was ready to sell the 41 percent of the company she had inherited from Edsel if Henry II was not immediately made president. The threat of outsider ownership within his empire served to focus the elder Henry's mind. He finally agreed to resign the presidency in favor of his grandson.

Immediately after the board meeting at which this happened, John Bugas, Henry II's aide, went to Bennett's office and told him to leave. In a scene right out of film noir (which was just then becoming popular), Bennett pulled .45 out of his desk drawer. Bugas drew the gun he had stuck in his belt and said, "Don't make the mistake of pulling the trigger, Harry, because I'll put one right through your heart." Bennett thought for a moment and put the .45 away. He cleaned out his desk by the end of the day and vanished.

When old Henry, now demented and totally divorced from the company that had been his life's work and obsession, died in his sleep in 1947, Henry II was in full control. He set out doggedly to make himself an auto man and earn his inheritance.

His problems were daunting. He needed not just to bring Ford back from the dead as a modern corporation, but also to keep it as a family business. He had inherited enough of his grandfather's genes to view outside control as unthinkable. So he had to create a supply of talented executives without letting any one of them gain enough power to threaten his ultimate control.

He bought in the so-called Whiz Kids, ten young former Air Force officers who had revolutionized strategic bombing during the war by treating it like a business. Several would become high-ranking executives at Ford, notable among them Robert McNamara, future Secretary of Defense. But, practicing balance of power politics to assure his leadership, Henry also brought in Ernest Breech, a former high-level GM executive who slowly began to modernize Ford's corporate structure according to the GM model.

Breech convinced Henry II that the company had to come up with something new quickly or it would be dead in the water. Henry II agreed to bet everything on a crash program to produce the 1949 Ford, a futuristic design containing a number of innovations Edsel had tried to implement 15 years earlier—an independent front suspension, a revamped transmission, and overdrive. When Henry II introduced it at the Waldorf Astoria in the summer of 1948, it created a sensation. Over 800,000 were sold in its first year, and this success guaranteed Ford's survival.

Henry II later said that the company was mother, wife, and mistress. His brothers also felt this umbilical connection and took roles at Ford, assuming that they too would be allowed to make serious bids for power. But there could only be one Ford in the driver's seat at a time. Over the next few years, Henry II made sure that Benson never became more than a ceremonial figure in the Lincoln Mercury division of which he was nominally in charge. And when Bill tried to advance via product design—he conceived the elegant Lincoln Continental Mark II as an homage to their father and as a car that would illustrate the company's dedication to quality—Henry II allowed his newly empowered, cost-conscious executives to block his brother's ambitions. Realizing that the route to the top was permanently blocked, Bill left Ford's daily operations, bought the Detroit Lions football team, and descended into a ten-year Lost Weekend.

Henry II defied the expectations of Detroit insiders by remaking Ford into a fully competitive company in the 1950s. The industry was continuing to consolidate: Kaiser and Frazier came and went; Nash and Hudson combined and disappeared; Packard picked up Studebaker and morphed into American Motors. In the midst of this shakeout, there appeared a cornucopia of buyer delights—cars with rocket-like bodies in sweet pastels, erotically bulging grilles, artifact hood ornaments, finny tails, and floating rides.

Ford and GM began a war of industrial espionage in the 1950s: They were spying on each other's proving grounds with telescopic cameras, planting agents in each other's design studios. For every punch there was a counterpunch. When Ford agents reported seeing an early version of the Corvette, for instance, the company immediately answered with its own prototype of a classy "boulevard car"—the Thunderbird. The T-Bird outsold the Vet three to one.

But if the Ford Motor Company was to regain the number one position—an obsessive topic at executive luncheons—it had to get serious about mid- and upper-range cars, Edsel's old agenda that his father had so destructively blocked. The company might have 43 percent of the lower-priced vehicle market, but only 13 percent of the more profitable mid-sized market. The Mercury, which was never more than a slightly gussied-up Ford, was not the solution. After top-secret strategy sessions, it was decided to use the Thunderbird's profits to build a completely new car.

Guards were posted all around the design studio where the e-car ("e" for experimental) was being developed. There was an exhaustive search for names, with Corsair, Citation, and Ranger among the final candidates. But in the end, the executives—against the instincts of the Ford family themselves—pushed for calling it the Edsel.

What was supposed to be a homage—ironic because the man who had borne that name had always hated it—turned out to be a disaster. When the Edsel was unveiled, critics said that the car's ungainly parts were out of synch, that it looked like a bastard child sired by many different fathers. After three years and more than $400 million in investments, the car was discontinued—and the name became a synonym for a huge failure of concept and marketing. The dream of going head to head with GM with all stalls fully occupied was now dead forever.

It was a setback, but the company was able to absorb it and so was Henry II. In fact, he was so much in control that he was able to tolerate strong executive personalities. In 1960, he moved up to CEO and made Robert McNamara, one of original postwar Whiz Kids, the first president of the Ford Motor Company who was not a family member. The ascetic McNamara was a "bean-counter," an industry swear word, not a natural car man. He killed the classy Thunderbird, which he regarded as part of the excesses of the 1950s. And before John F. Kennedy snatched him away for the cabinet, he scored a triumph by introducing the parsimonious Falcon. The Falcon competed with the surprisingly popular VW bug and was marketed as a second car for families now able, for the first time, to afford that luxury.

The next big executive personality at Ford was Semon Knudsen, known as "Bunkie." He was almost as much a part of Detroit's "gasoline aristocracy" as Henry Ford himself. His father, William Knudsen, had worked for the first Henry until the old man fired him for being too creative. Knudsen senior got his revenge by moving to GM and becoming president of Chevrolet in the mid-1920s, just as Chevys began leaving Fords in the dust. Like his father, Bunkie had come up through GM, having headed Pontiac where he and John DeLorean brought out one of the most popular muscle cars. In 1968, Knudsen was head of GM Overseas Operations (GMOO) when Henry Ford II brought him in as the new president of the Ford Motor Company. But the minute he arrived, he ran into a buzzsaw named Lee Iacocca.

"*I* am the product man in this company," Iacocca said upon hearing that Knudsen had been named president. "*I* move the iron." It was true: In his rise through the company in the 1950s and 1960s, Lee Iacocca had established himself as the greatest car man of his day, the man who brought us the Mustang, one of the great cars. Iacocca was also Machiavellian: His scheming was so swift and deadly that Knudsen never knew what hit him, and he was forced to leave Ford after only a year in office. "The first Henry Ford said that history is bunk," some unnamed Ford executive quipped upon hearing of the firing. "Now Bunkie is history."

To punish him for his out-of-control ambition, Henry Ford made Iacocca wait for a year before making him president. When he finally did take over, he added value with the Maverick, Fiesta and other models, including the Pinto (though he quickly disavowed paternity, attributing it to Henry when it became evident that the car caught fire if rear ended) and the Lincoln Continental Mark III. This version of the classic had none of elegance of its predecessors, which were done by Edsel and Bill Ford; in fact, according to some critics, it looked like "a Mafia staff car." But it outsold the Cadillac El Dorado and allowed Iacocca to note triumphantly that the Lincoln division had turned its first profit since Henry Ford bought the name back in 1921.

All of Iacocca's accomplishments reflected well on Henry II, who was, in midlife, an epic figure in Detroit—"Hank the Deuce," a gravelly voiced, gruff, no-nonsense man of power and the auto world's most visible symbol. In 1973, on the 30th anniversary of his taking control of the company, *Fortune* magazine published a cover story titled "Henry Ford, Superstar." It celebrated him as an industrial statesman, a community leader, and a political insider. He was the first man since his grandfather to have such clout. Although unlike his grandfather in that he was allergic to big ideas, particularly those unconnected to automobiles, Henry II resembled his namesake in that he did things his way. At the height of his power, he left his wife of 25 years and engaged in a very public affair with an Italian woman named Christina Vettore. He pursued *la dolce vita* in Italy, hanging out with Gianni Angelli and other Italian automakers. Stories of his wild and indulgent lifestyle soon became a tabloid staple. Henry II answered their critiques with the phrase that became his credo: "Never complain, never explain."

But amidst his success were disquieting signs in the industry, warnings of another paradigm shift symbolized by the formation of OPEC, lines at gas stations, and most of all by a new kind of competition from abroad. Now it was not just Volkswagen with its new Rabbit that he had to worry about, but Honda with its Civic, and Toyota and Datsun.

Mistakenly assuming that this was just another blip on the screen, executives at Ford and GM rushed out the Pinto and the Vega to compete, just as they had done with the Falcon and the Corvair when the economy craze hit in the 1960s. What they missed was that in the mid-1970s economy and fuel efficiency were not the consumers' only concerns: They wanted quality as well. Buyers were beginning to say that they were fed up with what Detroit produced, and that they were ready for something different. Because the auto industry was cocooned in the denial that persists to this day, what began as a protest became a permanent change of habit. Except in Michigan, perhaps, it was no longer un-American to buy a non-American car.

Henry II was like the others in that he ignored the early warning signs of this shift in the industry's tectonic plates. But he couldn't ignore Lee Iacocca, who continued to inflate his already larger-than-life persona every day, letting it be known that the company would probably be better off if he had all the power. The growing enmity between the two men was masked by arguments about products—whether to introduce a new generation of small front-wheel-drive cars, whether to produce the revolutionary minivan—when it was really all about personality. Because of his own background, Iacocca couldn't help but see Henry as a spoiled rich guy who had been handed everything on a silver platter. Because of his traumatic past, Henry II couldn't help but see Iacocca as Harry Bennett all over again.

The conflict, which riveted the auto world in the years it simmered and the wider public when it finally came to a boil, took on existential implications for Henry in 1976 when he had a heart attack. Who would replace him if he died? His brother Benson, made irrelevant at Ford, was killing himself with booze. His other brother Bill, who had courageously beaten the bottle, had a car man's instincts, but had been little more than a casual board member in the years since his ambitions at Ford had been blocked. The next generation—especially Henry's son Edsel II and Bill's son Billy—was not ready yet. In any case Henry had made it clear at the occasional Ford family meetings that the business was much more complex than it had been when he took over—and that the Ford Motor Company could no longer afford to have Crown Princes.

In 1978, to block Iacocca's efforts, Henry formed an Executive Office, the top of the Ford power pyramid, which included himself, Iacocca, and Philip Caldwell. Iacocca got the message and immediately went on the attack. Caldwell, he said, was a nobody—even though Caldwell had been a huge success as head of Ford International, whose profits accounted for nearly half of the company's income. Iacocca also attacked Henry Ford II.

No one other than Lee Iacocca would have dared try to stage a palace coup against the biggest name in the auto business. But he began to plot, aided by a clique of Ford directors who were part of his fan club. The months' long conflict with Henry was like a heavy-weight slugging match. It finally came to a head at the mid-year board meeting in 1978, when some of the directors said they planned to ask for Iacocca's reinstatement as head man. Henry told them, "It's he or me. You have 30 minutes to make up your minds. If you don't give me a vote of confidence, I'll resign. Think about how that will look in tomorrow's *Wall Street Journal.*"

He got his vote and summoned Iacocca to his office the next day to tell him he was through. Iacocca wanted to know why, although the answer was obvious. Henry looked down at him over his reading glasses for a moment and said, "Well, sometimes you just don't like somebody."

Some observers compared what had happened at Ford to Michael Corleone straightening things out at the end of *The Godfather.* Having taken care of the family's business, Henry retired as chairman and CEO in 1980 and named Philip Caldwell to both positions. He went on a slow-motion, three-year trip to all the plants and headquarters around the world that made up the vast Ford empire, a long goodbye to those who had worked for him over half a lifetime. People compared him to his grandfather, noting that while the first Henry had breathed life into a great company, the second had revived it from its industrial coma. But Henry II refused to be bookended with his grandfather. Asked by a reporter why he had squandered his life in the trenches at Ford, Henry II's response showed, as we used to say in the 1960s, how much the personal is political. "I did it for my father," he answered. "I wanted to show the world that my father's seed was strong. I *remember* my father!"

On his way out the door, Iacocca had snarled that Ford would never again see a profit like the $1.5 billion he had racked up during his last year at the helm. But, in fact, the 1980s were a good time for the company. The leadership team Henry had put in place upon leaving—Philip Caldwell and his second-in-command Donald Petersen—made record profits: $1.9 billion in 1983, $2.9 billion the following year, reaching $3.3 billion in 1986, when the company beat GM for the first time since 1924. During this period, the up-styled Ford Taurus and Mercury Sable were named the best American cars. From his new perch as head of Chrysler, where the grapes were very sour, Iacocca scornfully described them as "flying potatoes."

When Henry II died in 1987, there was no state funeral such as marked his grandfather's passing, when over 100,000 people filed through the Henry Ford Museum to see the old man's body lying in state. But Henry II's death marked something more profound—the end of an epic intergenerational tale of creativity and destruction, genius and madness, guilt and redemption, and an awesome industrial power once concentrated now beginning to leak away.

As it worked out, there was another Ford in the company's future—young Bill. He had won out after a decade-long rivalry with Henry's son Edsel II, which had faint echoes of the Oedipal struggles of previous generations. Bill rose to the CEO position in 1999 by his considerable talents as well as the support of the vast bloc of voting stock that made the 81-member Ford family more equal than other stockholders.

He is a kinder, gentler Ford—a liberal on social issues and a committed environmentalist, who, while not exactly pulling himself up by his bootstraps, had nonetheless earned his spurs by doing time in a 20-year apprenticeship in every corner of the company. He too wanted to put a personal stamp on the Ford Motor Company, and he talked bravely of greening the company. But he allowed Ford to get seduced by the success of SUVs in the late 1990s. As a result, it was unprepared to deal with the clamor about fuel standards and the rise in gas prices.

When Bill stepped back from leadership in 2006 in favor of former Boeing head Alan Mulally, it made big news in the financial pages. But for dedicated Ford-watchers this was just the final evanescence of the tail of a comet that had already passed by years earlier. The question was no longer who would be the next Ford in the company. Those days were over. The question now was whether Ford, still the symbol of the American auto industry even in its decline, could recreate itself one more time.

MARTIN FRIDSON

Do Ethanol Regulations Make Sense?

Ethanol is a gasoline substitute produced from biomass. In the United States, the usual raw material for ethanol is corn. Familiar to students of organic chemistry as C_9H_5OH, ethanol is a colorless, volatile, and flammable liquid. The substance is also known as grain alcohol. Interestingly, ethanol has also been described as one of earliest recreational drugs.

Lacking a degree in chemistry or proficiency in substance abuse, the only connection I have with ethanol is a loose one. I am an investment manager specializing in high yield bonds. The press refers to these securities as "junk bonds," based on an above-average probability that the issuer will go bankrupt and default on its obligations.

An issuer in this market that produces ethanol, Verasun, recently did exactly that. While I am proud to say my company never went anywhere near those bonds, their existence within our investable universe requires us at least to be familiar with the ethanol industry.

In my 2006 book, *Unwarranted Intrusions: The Case Against Government Intervention in the Marketplace*,[1] I wrote about ethanol. This book established me as an expert of sorts on subsidies in areas such as programs that promote savings, athletic stadiums, the arts—and agricultural products, including ethanol. But the ethanol story has taken many strange twists since *Unwarranted Intrusions* was published, so further research was necessary to update my knowledge.

Amazing Parallels with Snake Oil

Based on what I already knew, my professional judgment was that the best place to start supplementary research on ethanol was to read up on snake oil. This turned out to be an excellent strategy.

Let me share a few passages from the *Wikipedia* article on snake oil. These excerpts capture effectively the key points I want to make about snake oil's modern equivalent—ethanol.

Wikipedia defines snake oil as follows:

> A derogatory term for compounds offered as medicines, which implies that they are fake, fraudulent, quackish, or ineffective. The expression is also applied metaphorically to any product with exaggerated marketing, but questionable or unverifiable quality or benefit.... [T]he archetype of hoax.

So the first point about ethanol is that it does not do what its promoters claim it does, which is to provide an environmentally friendly, cost-effective substitute for gasoline that can free the United States from its dependence on imported oil.

The second point about ethanol: It *will* run a car.

The idea that biomass, such as corn, can be an energy source is not unfounded. The question is, does burning corn to run motor vehicles represent an effective use of resources, or is it a scheme to funnel money to corporations and segments of the population with disproportionate political influence? For the time being, I will leave you in suspense about which side I come down on.

Here is something you probably did not know about snake oil, quoting again from *Wikipedia*:

> Snake oil is still used as a pain reliever in China. Fats and oils from snakes are higher in eicosapentaenoic acid (EPA) than other sources, so snake oil was actually a plausible remedy for joint pain as these are thought to have inflammation-reducing properties.

But there was just one small problem when it comes to snake oil sold by patent medicine salesmen of the Old West:

> American snake fats do not have EPA contents as high as those of the Chinese water snake. The American snake oils were not effective in relieving pain like the original Chinese snake oil—further promoting the hoax stereotype.

So here is one more parallel: Today's purveyors of ethanol, like old-time snake oil salesmen, take advantage of the fact that not every voter will amass all the scientific knowledge necessary to make an informed judgment about the value of a product. This is a fundamental problem of democracy, which nevertheless remains the best system of government devised so far.

Let me note one other important aspect of the ethanol program: When ethanol is discredited as a solution for one problem, its promoters simply present is as a solution to another problem in order to keep the subsidy spigot flowing. If the fuel-efficiency story gets discredited, ethanol becomes the solution to air pollution. If it turns out that ethanol harms, rather than helps, the environment, it becomes a weapon in the war on terrorism.

Once again, this aspect of ethanol has a parallel in the history of snake oil:

> Snake fat also played a role in ancient Egyptian medicine, mixed with the fats of lion, hippopotamus, crocodile, tomcat, and Nubian ibex into a homogenous mass believed to cause bald men to grow hair.

In short, whatever the problem, snake oil—or ethanol—is the solution.

Let me offer one final point about ethanol illuminated by this aspect of my research. I have been talking about snake oil, a substance that gained prominence in the United States back in the nineteenth century. As we shall see, ethanol as an automobile fuel is not a recent innovation; it has a longer history than most voters realize.

As *Wikipedia* states, in yet another close parallel with ethanol:

> The practice of selling dubious remedies for real (or imagined) ailments still occurs today, albeit with some updated marketing techniques.

Ethanol, too, has proven hard to dismiss from the nation's fuel mix because its advocates are exceedingly clever.

History of the Ethanol Subsidy

The history of ethanol as an automobile fuel actually goes back further than snake oil in the U.S., which was introduced in the mid-nineteenth century by Chinese laborers who were constructing the transcontinental railroad.

In 1826 Samuel Morey developed an internal combustion engine that ran on ethanol and turpentine. Furthermore, Henry Ford's very first car, an 1896 quadricycle, was built to run on pure ethanol.

Gasoline quickly became the dominant auto fuel, but shortages during World War I stimulated demand for ethanol. The alternative fuel also was popular in World War II and in-between, during the Great Depression, when ethanol blends gained some traction in the Midwest. But under normal market conditions, ethanol has never been competitive with gasoline.

If a product fails decade after decade in a free-enterprise system, that ought to settle the question of its viability for our great corporations. After all, the CEOs of these companies love to extol the virtues of free enterprise and complain about government interference. Strangely, though, this fine talk about free markets does not prevent companies from lobbying aggressively for trade protection or public financing for private ventures.

If you are a company looking for a handout from the government, it helps to have friends in both major parties. Dwayne Andreas of the food processing giant Archer Daniels Midland (ADM) was a master of working both sides of the aisle. He referred to the practice as "slopping both hogs." Here are a few things Dwayne Andreas did to win political friendships:

In 1992, Andreas, combined with his family and ADM, was the largest contributor to the Republican Party; in the same year, he ranked third among Democratic contributors. Andreas underwrote military school education for Democratic Vice President Hubert Humphrey's children. When Republican Senate Majority Leader Bob Dole's wife became the head of the Red Cross, Andreas's foundation coughed up a $1 million contribution to that fine organization. Then there was the visit Andreas made to President Richard Nixon in 1972. Nixon's secretary later recalled that the purpose of the visit was to deliver $100,000 in $100 bills. One year later, with the heat turned up on the Watergate scandal, Nixon gave the money back.

In fact, Andreas was so eager to be a good friend that he did more than was asked. And he did more than was legal, resulting in his having to pay a fine in 1993 for exceeding the limits on campaign contributions. Andreas was not embarrassed about giving money to politicians. He likened it to tithing.

Consequently, in 1978 Dwayne Andreas was in a good position to persuade President Jimmy Carter that it was vital to our nation's interests for the taxpayers to subsidize a product that had been failing in the marketplace for 80 years. This dismal performance record was of no consequence to Andreas. What mattered to him was that ethanol was produced by Archer Daniels Midland. Today it is the single largest contributor to the company's profits. By the way, Andreas's coziness with politicians earned ADM the Cato Institute's designation as "the most prominent recipient of corporate welfare in recent history."[2]

Andreas's hard work paid off with more than just accolades. The Energy Tax Act of 1978 exempted all blends of gasoline that contained at least 10 percent ethanol from the 4-cent-per-gallon federal gasoline excise tax. In effect, this amounted to a 40-cent-per-gallon subsidy for ethanol. And that was just the camel's nose under the tent. Lobbyists quickly went to work expanding the levels of government support. Thanks to their efforts, the ethanol subsidy rose from 40 cents a gallon to 50 cents in 1983 and 60 cents in 1984.

In 1980, Congress authorized insured loans for ethanol producers. That same year, a tariff on foreign-produced ethanol became law. Currently, the tariff is 54 cents a gallon—a rate designed to offset the 51-cent federal tax credit for all ethanol, regardless of where it is produced.

This trade barrier is highly significant because unlike corn-based ethanol produced in the United States, Brazilian ethanol is made from sugarcane, and it is actually economical without any subsidy. Brazilian distillers can produce ethanol for 22 cents a liter, versus 30 cents a liter for U.S. distillers. The difference in production costs reflects the simple fact that cornstarch must be converted into sugar before being distilled into alcohol; the Brazilians' process *starts* with sugar. In light of this insuperable cost advantage, Federal Reserve Chairman Ben Bernanke has testified that it would be helpful to remove the tariff on Brazilian ethanol.

A natural question is, "If ethanol is so good for the environment, why put a tariff on it, which makes it more expensive and less likely to be used?" I saw Senator Dick Durbin of Illinois answer this question on television by resorting to the infant industry argument. This is a classic notion in economic theory that protection from foreign competition is justified when an industry is just getting started. That is a plausible idea, but ethanol has been around as an auto fuel for over 100 years! The only new thing is the use of tax dollars to make a "success" of a product that has failed miserably, and repeatedly, in the marketplace.

An alternative explanation was offered by C. Ford Runge, an economist specializing in commodities and trade policy at the Center for International Food and Agricultural Policy at University of Minnesota. Runge says an "obvious thing to do" is to lower the 54-cent tariff and let some Brazilian ethanol into U.S. But he acknowledges that "one of the fundamental reasons biofuels policy is so out of whack with markets and reality is that interest group politics have been so dominant in the construction of the subsidies that support it."[3]

One aspect of the U.S. ethanol program that does make sense, from a certain point of view, is the increasing size of ethanol subsidies. The tax breaks have to get bigger and bigger, because the government's own research shows that making ethanol from corn is uneconomical.

According to the Agriculture Department, a gallon of ethanol contains only two-thirds as much energy as a gallon of gasoline. Given that the industry's main blend, gasohol, is 10 percent ethanol, using ethanol reduces gas mileage by 3.3 percent. Moreover, Energy Department analysts say that in practice, this figure is optimistic. Note that if gas mileage declines when we replace gasoline with a blend of gasoline and ethanol, it undercuts the argument that using ethanol reduces oil imports.

Furthermore, in 1991 the Energy Department estimated that taking into account all the energy required to run an ethanol plant, as well as that used to grow, harvest, and ship corn, it requires 85,000 to 90,000 Btus to produce one gallon of ethanol containing the energy equivalent of 76,000 Btus. Therefore, doing the math shows that ethanol makes our imported oil problem worse, not better.

To be fair, this is a hotly contested point, and the numbers cited in the Energy Department study are average figures. At a minimum, though, it does seem clear that it is energy-inefficient to produce ethanol in drier corn-growing areas, where crops must be irrigated with pumps than run on natural gas.

What about ethanol's supposed environmental benefits? In reality, environmentalists are among the strongest critics of ethanol. For instance, the Sierra Club concludes that ethanol decreases the creation of carbon monoxide, but *increases* smog by stepping up the evaporation of the gasoline with which it is mixed.

The Green Party's 2002 candidate for Governor of Minnesota said that ethanol production would require corn to be cultivated under conditions requiring massive doses of chemicals and resulting in soil erosion. Other research shows mixing ethanol and gasoline can increase emissions of acetaldehyde, a toxic pollutant, and also aggravate seepage of benzene and other toxins into groundwater. The overall conclusion of the Energy Department was that there are no significant environmental benefits to gasohol.

There is a further problem. Even with a subsidy, it turns out that ethanol production is profitable only when corn is cheap. As with any other commodity, corn prices are sometimes high, sometimes low. One bout of high corn prices in the 1980s drove the majority of ethanol producers out of business.

If this business fails not only in the free market but also with a government subsidy, you would think the conclusion would be that it is time to throw in the towel on ethanol. But no! The ethanol lobby managed to insert a new sort of preference into the Energy Policy Act of 1992, which required certain automobile fleets to purchase vehicles capable of running on alternative fuels. Conveniently, E-85—a blend of 15 percent gasoline and 85 percent ethanol—qualified as one of those alternative fuels. Meanwhile, the subsidy for gasohol continued, albeit at a slightly reduced rate because of lower oil prices. By 2004, the federal ethanol subsidy was costing taxpayers

$1.4 billion annually, despite a resounding lack of consumer enthusiasm for the fuel.

Still, the government's assistance ramped up further. In 2005, for the first time, Washington required refiners to blend ethanol into a portion of their gasoline output. New legislation called for 7.5 billion gallons of renewable fuel to be added to the annual U.S. fuel supply by 2012. In 2007, the Energy Independence and Security Act increased the ethanol mandate to 15 billion gallons per year by 2015.

While all this was happening at the federal level, the states got into the act. When a poor corn crop again caused prices to surge in 1995 to 1996, several states came to the rescue of the ethanol producers that had not gone bust in the cost squeeze of a decade earlier.

Keep in mind, price swings in agricultural commodities are not exactly extraordinary, unforeseeable acts of God that would seem to justify government intervention. Nevertheless, the ethanol lobby has repeatedly proven itself powerful enough to shield ethanol producers from ordinary business risk.

By this point, some of you must be deploring the dishonesty of it all. The ethanol subsidy, including mandated usage for some autos, is being presented as something it is not. Ethanol is not a solution to the U.S.'s dependence on foreign oil, and it is not a form of clean energy. Is there no honest politician out there?

I am pleased to tell you that there *is* one honest politician. His name is Ben Nelson, a senator from Nebraska, which happens to be a major corn and ethanol producing state. The following is Nelson's statement about why American needs to subsidize ethanol, citing no foreign oil sheiks or clean air promises:

> We have an obligation to help agriculture get on its feet. There have always been enough tax benefits to go around for virtually everybody. That's the way the system works to promote the economy.[4]

There's honesty for you. Everyone else is getting a subsidy, so by golly the farmers in my state are going to get one, too. And if you think there used to be more honesty in politics than there is now, you are right. A number of politicians, such as Hillary Clinton, used to be *against* ethanol subsidies—until they ran for president.

Externalities

To address fully the question of whether ethanol subsidies make sense, we also have to look at the hidden costs involved. These costs are not limited to reducing tax revenue to help supposedly beleaguered farmers. Burning corn as fuel increases demand for corn, which is exactly what farmers want. But under the law of supply and demand, conjuring up new demand for corn also boosts the price of corn and the cost of food derived from corn, including meat produced from corn-fed livestock.

This is not just a U.S. problem. The Organization for Economic Cooperation and Development warned in July 2008 that growth in biofuels production would drive up food prices and contribute to "food insecurity for the most vulnerable populations in developing countries," yet have a "limited impact on reducing greenhouse gases and improving energy security."[5]

Similarly, a July 2008 World Bank report blamed a big increase in biofuels production for rising fuel prices that imposed particular hardship on poor people in developing countries. In some of these poorer nations, rising costs led to food riots.

Back here at home, the USDA says that without biofuels production raising the cost of corn-fed animals that provide milk, meat, and eggs, food inflation might be 0.7 percentage points lower. A Purdue University study showed that biofuels production accounted for two-thirds of food price inflation in 2007, or the equivalent of $15 billion.

Naturally, ethanol enthusiast Tom Daschle, the former Senate Majority Leader, prefers studies such as the one released by the White House Council of Economic Advisers, which concluded that ethanol production is responsible for only 2 or 3 percent of the rise in global food prices. These economists blamed the bulk of food price increases on higher costs for energy, transportation, and fertilizer.

However, Keith Collins, former chief economist for the USDA, concluded that the White House estimate of a 2 to 3 percent contribution by ethanol omitted the impact on crops other than corn. For instance, higher corn prices give farmers an incentive to shift acreage from wheat to corn, so wheat prices rise as supply declines. Collins estimated that biofuels contributed not 2 or 3 percent of inflation in food prices, but rather 23 to 35 percent, or more than ten times the government number.

The impact on corn prices became such a big issue for livestock ranchers in 2008 that Texas Governor Rick Perry petitioned the Environmental Protection Agency to cut its 9 million gallon ethanol mandate for 2008 by 50 percent. The EPA is authorized to waive the mandate if it causes "severe harm" to the economy, yet Perry's petition was rejected. Environmental regulators acknowledged that high commodity prices were having an economic impact, but found "no compelling evidence" of severe harm.

Effects such as this documented spillover to food prices are known to economists as "externalities." And ethanol's externalities are not limited to increased food prices. For instance, new studies question whether ethanol burns more cleanly than other types of gasoline. A recent study by Mark Jacobson, a Stanford University civil and environmental engineering professor, found that increased use of ethanol could lead to a rise in the number of cases of severe respiratory illness.[6]

In addition, shifting acreage to corn cultivation reduces the populations of beetles and other insects that prey on aphids, the number one soybean pest in the United States. Douglas Landis and research colleagues at Michigan State University calculated that in Iowa, Michigan, Minnesota, and Wisconsin, the cost to soybean producers in terms of lower yields and increased pesticide needs approaches $60 million per year.[7]

Finally, mechanics who work on boats, motorcycles, and lawnmowers blame the ethanol blend E10 for an increase in engine problems. This is because it is not uncommon to leave fuel in the tanks of such seasonal vehicles and equipment untouched for two months or more. Over time ethanol attracts water, which dilutes the fuel and makes engines hard to start. Along with that inconvenience, some consumers spend extra time obtaining small amounts of pure gasoline to reap the benefits of higher mileage relative to blends. These search costs represent yet another cost imposed by subsidization of ethanol.

Moral Objection

Now, I realize not everything in life is a matter of dollars and cents. Many of us believe there is a higher morality than our pocketbooks. It turns out, however, that we can be offended by the ethanol program on moral as well as financial grounds.

Bloomberg News recently wrote about a Minnesota farmer hooking a pump to a grain silo and drawing out enough corn to feed 91 people for one year. Instead, that corn will be turned into enough ethanol to fuel vehicles in the city of Houston for 21 seconds. The *Bloomberg* article pointed out that in the 1930s some people considered it a sin to burn corn in home furnaces. Said the mayor of Luverne, Minnesota: "They felt it was a food, and there's always hungry people in the world."

Meanwhile, Korean farmer Park Ho Kon saw the cost of feed jump 70 percent in 2008. "The rest of the world is suffering from famine, but the U.S. is making fuel from corn. Well, isn't that a powerful country's logic."[9]

Yet another thing to get incensed about is the strain that ethanol production puts on the world's water supply. By one estimate, the amount of water needed to produce biofuels for one SUV's gas tank equals the amount required to feed one person with grains for an entire year. There is plenty of room for moral outrage about ethanol.

Putting the Thumb Down on the Scale

One more reason to object to the ethanol subsidy program is that it is a case of government favoring one particular technology over potentially superior alternatives. Investors rush to a government-favored technology like moths to a flame, arming stock promoters with a powerful pitch to raise money for new ventures. Such ventures are fundamentally unsound, however, if the fuel is competitive only with the help of a massive taxpayer subsidy. One day taxpayers are likely to stand up and say, "No more!"

We have recently witnessed a dramatic demonstration of the dangers of investing on the premise of government favoritism. On October 22, 2008, the *Financial Times* reported that six of the largest publicly traded U.S. ethanol producers had collectively lost $8.7 billion market value since the industry's mid-2006 peak; some stocks fell 90 percent. One prominent loser was Cascade Investments, the private investment firm of Microsoft founder Bill Gates, which lost several million dollars on Pacific Ethanol Inc.

The ethanol boom and subsequent ethanol bust resulted directly from 2005 legislation that required refiners to blend billions of gallons of ethanol with gasoline. Tax subsidies from that point through

the beginning October 2008 exceeded the amount lost by investors by
$2.5 billion.

There is nothing inherently wrong with investors losing money in
the stock market. Risk is an essential ingredient in any successful capitalist system. Despite the recent trend toward bailouts in almost every
sector of the economy, it is *not* conducive to an efficient allocation of
resources for the government to indemnify investors against losses.

By the same token, it is not sound policy for government to go
out and create losses where they would not otherwise occur. Without
government subsidies, venture capitalists might have risked some money
on the possibility of a technological breakthrough that would make
ethanol cost-competitive with gasoline. But without such an advance
in the laboratory, these startup ventures never would have gone public
and therefore would not have put individual and institutional investors
in a position to lose $8.7 billion.

There is a better way to subsidize development of alternative
energy—if that is even necessary. There is plenty of incentive to conduct
research. Anybody who develops and retains ownership of a process
to domestically produce energy that is environmentally safe and competitive with fossil fuels can count on entering the Forbes 400 list, the
bottom rung of which is now greater than $1 billion.

Let us assume, however, that it can be satisfactorily demonstrated
that the necessary technological advances will not occur without subsidization. In that case, let taxpayers pay for *results*, instead of throw-
ing money at technologies that already have huge amounts of capital
committed to them and therefore lots of lobbying muscle, but which
are not assured of ever becoming cost-competitive with oil. The question is: Why should government put its thumb down on the scale on
behalf of existing technologies that may prove inferior to others still
to be developed?

A better approach would be to offer a bounty to anyone who
comes up with any technology—biofuel, solar, windpower—that
legitimately meets the test of cost-competitiveness with conventional
fuels. Let inventors, engineers, and entrepreneurs calculate the odds
on which approaches have the best chance of paying off. Congress is
not really equipped to make those estimates.

Outlook under New Administration

Just in case you are expecting the new administration to provide change you can believe in, don't count on it when it comes to ethanol. President Obama comes from a major corn-producing state and he voted for the 2007 farm bill that mandated an increase in ethanol production, whether consumers want the stuff or not. Obama does not appear to be a fan of using ethanol produced in the most cost-effective way: During his presidential campaign he said, "It does not serve our national and economic security to replace imported oil with Brazilian ethanol."

The new president's cabinet includes several members with similar backgrounds and viewpoints. In fact, the Washington newsletter *The Hill* calls Obama's cabinet a "dream team for ethanol." The only way the cabinent could have been more pro-ethanol was if Tom Daschle's nomination for Health and Human Services Secretary had not been derailed. Daschle actually received an award in 2005 from the American Coalition for Ethanol.

Within the cabinet, the only encouraging sign is some support for developing ethanol from biomass sources other than corn, a potentially more environmentally friendly approach. Currently, the primary proposed alternative is switchgrass, also known as tall panic grass, Wobsqua grass, lowland switchgrass, blackbent, tall prairiegrass, wild redtop, and thatchgrass. By whichever name, switchgrass is usually grown as ground cover or for forage for animals. Also promising, in a related area, is stinkweed as a potential source of biodiesel, or home heating oil made from soybeans and other food crops.

In addition, there are some encouraging signs on other side of aisle, even though historically interference in the market to support handouts for ethanol producers has been a bipartisan effort. The 2008 Republican platform called for an end to the mandate for increased production of renewable fuels, even though President George W. Bush supported the mandate. Observers saw the hand of John McCain in the anti-mandate plank. McCain has bought the story of ethanol as antidote to global warming, but to his credit the Arizona senator has consistently opposed subsidies. Encouragingly, too, Representative Jeff Flake (R–AZ) has introduced H.R. 5911, the Remove Incentives for Producing Ethanol Act of 2008, which would eliminate the mandate and other benefits for ethanol. Similar measures may soon be introduced.

Summary

Earlier I compared subsidized ethanol to snake oil, a generic term for medicines that are ineffective or fraudulent. That analogy may offend some. To those who object to my pointing out parallels between snake oil and ethanol, let me offer my sincere and profound refusal to apologize.

This essay posed the question: Does burning corn to run ethanol plants represent an effective use of resources or a scheme to funnel money to corporations and segments of the population with disproportionate political influence? I believe the evidence clearly shows that taxpayer-subsidized ethanol is *not* an efficient use of resources. It *is* a highly effective method of steering government funds to powerful economic interests through the exertions of skilled lobbyists.

To the question posed by my title—"Do Ethanol Regulations Make Sense?"—I give a two-part answer.

As an economic proposition, the answer is an emphatic *no*. Subsidies are not justified by any benefit in the form of replacement of imported oil, given the energy required to produce and transport ethanol. Subsidies are not justified by a reduction of the greenhouse effect—ethanol production may instead *increase* carbon dioxide production overall. On the cost side, biofuels production makes food more costly and harms the environment through such effects as increased pesticide use and strains on finite water supplies.

As a proposition to benefit special interests, the answer to the same question, whether ethanol regulations make sense, is an equally emphatic *yes*. Ethanol subsidies make lots of sense for farmers and corn processors. It is a plain and simple transfer of wealth to them from other segments of society, cloaked under false claims of gains to the environment and national security. Paradoxically, the bigger failure the program is, the more Congress increases the subsidy.

Despite its many flaws, the ethanol program survives because information dissemination is imperfect. I believe that anyone who has an objective viewpoint and can afford the time to study the matter will arrive at the same conclusion that I have. After 80 years of marketplace failure, corn-based ethanol should not be propped up into an artificial success with our tax dollars.

ETHANOL-WAYS

Music by Irving Berlin
Lyrics by Marty Fridson
Arrangement by Daniel Fridson
Performed by Winnie Nip

You'll burn ethanol always,
Summer, winter, fall, always.
When there's scant demand,
Uncle Sam will understand
Lend a helping hand,

Always.

No one freely buys always,
So we'll subsidize always,
Not just one more year,
But forever more I fear,
Whether corn is cheap or dear.

Yes, always.

The video can be viewed at http://www.youtube.com/user/DFFProductions.

Notes

1. Martin Fridson, *Unwarranted Intrusions: The Case Against Government Intervention in the Marketplace* (Hoboken, NJ: John Wiley & Sons, 2006).
2. James Bovard, "Archer Daniels Midland: A Case Study in Corporate Welfare," *Cato Institute Policy Analysis, No. 241* (September 26, 1995): http://www.cato.org/pubs/pa-241.html, p.1.
3. Larry Rohter, "Ethanlol Industry Has Provided Obama with Some Top Advisers," *New York Times* (June 23, 2008: A-1.
4. Lizette Alvarez with David Barboza, "Support Grows for Corn-Based Fuel Despite Critics," *New York Times* (November 26, 2009): http://www.nytimes.com/2001/07/23/businesss/support-grows-for-corn-based-fuel-despite-critics.html.
5. Lauren Etter, "Ethanol Backers, Critics Ratchet Up the Rhetoric," *Wall Streeet Journal* (July 17, 2008): A4.
6. Mark Z. Jacobson, "Effects of Ethanol (E85) Versus Gasoline Vehicles on Cancer and Mortality in the United States," *Environmental Science and Technology* (in press).
7. Growing More Corn for Ethanol Makes Pest Control Harder," *New York Times* (December 23, 2008): D3.
8. Peter Robison, "Eating Isn't Option When Minnesota Corn Burns in Houston Cars," *Bloomberg News* (December 15, 2008): www.bloombergnews.com.
9. Ibid.

MYRON EBELL

New Car Technology:
Should Government Have a Role?

What role should government play in developing, or perhaps hindering, new automotive technology? To approach an answer, we must examine a few examples of the roles governments have played or are playing in developing car technology. That is to say, I am going to consider the question historically before trying to come to any sort of normative policy advice.

I cannot, however, conceal my prejudices in this matter. I work for a free market think tank, and I believe government should play little or no role in developing new auto technology. Keeping government hands off is in the best interest of the auto industry and of its consumers—and it also makes for much better government.

Someone who has spent his life in the automotive industry and has expertise in engineering and the like is going to know a lot more about what constitutes the right kind of car than someone sitting in an office in Washington. What complicates this, of course, is that we now live in a mixed economy: We are not really talking about our representatives in Congress deciding specifically what the auto industry should do. We are talking about a vast apparatus of research laboratories with government-funded research, cooperative projects, and regulatory agencies.

Aldous Huxley set his utopian novel *Brave New World* in the year A.F. 32—632 years after Henry Ford introduced the Model T. *Brave New World* was published in 1932, which was only 24 years A.F. We are now in the 101st year After Ford. I call attention to this because Huxley saw early on that the automobile would bring decisive changes to the planet. Huxley imagined a world that would eventually forsake Christianity and the ordering of history according to the birth of Jesus for a brave new era begun by Ford. You may recall that in the novel the tops of crosses were broken off so as to make the letter T. This is fanciful, but what Huxley foresaw was that the remarkable technological advances of our age could come to a very bad end. Technology could create a society that gives people what they want, or what they think they want: lives of effortless, meaningless pleasures without the bother of birth pains, or thinking, or love, or faith, or striving, or old age, or death. *Brave New World* is a disturbing picture of a post-Christian society in thrall to technology.

In the course of history few material advances have been as prized, or caused so much delight, as the mobility provided by automobiles. Americans are known throughout the world as being crazy about cars and the open road. People in every country and in every culture dream of owning a car. This fact reminds me that when John Steinbeck's novel *The Grapes of Wrath* was made into a movie by John Ford in 1940, the Soviet government was extremely eager to get a copy to show the people of Russia how awful life was for the proletariat in evil, capitalist, Depression-era America. Stalin's government began to show the movie, but then quickly decided to withdraw it. Why? Because it showed that in America even the poorest Okie in the Dust Bowl could own a car! Admittedly, it was a broken-down old jalopy, but it was a car, nevertheless.

This story suggests something fundamental about the nature of automobiles: their equalizing nature. Neither Communism, nor socialism, nor any other scheme for redistributing wealth has done as much to make people of all classes roughly equal in terms of their access to the material goods of life than has car ownership. Consider the differences among the classes before the automobile. For example, when the first Continental Congress was called in Philadelphia, Virginia slave owners came to Philadelphia in horse-drawn carriages. By contrast,

John Adams, a prosperous lawyer in Boston, travelled to Philadelphia by walking through the mud and rain. This kind of social divide is not present in America today.

The threat posed by mobility to the old regime in Europe was recognized very early on. For example, in the early nineteenth century the Duke of Wellington opposed the first railroads in England on the grounds that railroads encouraged needless movement by the common people. I wonder who gets to decide what constitutes "needless"? Similarly, modern totalitarian governments have taken extraordinary measures to limit the mobility of their subjects.

Now I don't mean to suggest that auto mobility is an unqualified good. For example, cars and highways have made it much easier for bank robbers to get away. This is a silly example, but it makes a serious point. Much more serious (and ominous) is the fact that the liberation brought about by automobiles and other new technology has tended to obscure the fact that in the twentieth century we have had a gradual loss of political liberty. This problem is not unique to the auto age: Ancient Greeks and Romans realized that material comfort is something that reconciles people to the gradual erosion of their political liberties.

From the time that coal-fired steam engines were first mounted on wheeled vehicles (as early as 1777 in France) until about the 1970s, the American government, and most governments in the free world, had a fairly consistent view of their proper role in terms of the advancement of automobile technology: Get out of the way—and stay out. There were some exceptions. From the beginning, the public complained about the danger, smoke, dust, and noise produced by automobiles. Government, therefore, had good reason to impose some rules of the road, such as speed limits, stop signs, and taillights.

I have been able to find only one major exception to this laissez-faire policy that dominated most Western countries until the 1970s. In 1836, the British House of Commons passed a very steep tax on steam coaches: They did this to put steam coaches out of business and to keep horse-drawn carriages in business. (The tax on steam coaches was approximately twelve times higher than that for horse-drawn carriages.) In 1865, the House of Commons passed the Red Flag Act, the result of lobbying by an unholy alliance of landed gentry and stagecoach and railway owners. The Red Flag law required every motorized vehicle to have at least three drivers and conductors, one of whom had to walk at least 60 yards in front of the vehicle waving a red flag and warning horse riders that a vehicle was approaching. It also set a maximum speed limit of four miles per hour. Amazingly, the Red Flag Act was not repealed by Parliament until 1896. James D. Johnston, a former Vice President of General Motors, quoted automobile historian E. H. Wakefield in his excellent book *Driving America*: "The Red Flag Act 'is one of the best documented examples of government regulation limiting progress, for by 1896 France was alight with the personal automobile.' In Great Britain, [Wakefield] wrote, 'the King's highways were largely limited to horses and horse-drawn liveries and conveyances.'"[1] This law, as crazy as it sounds, was a mild precursor to what we live with today.

During the two centuries that most governments stayed out of the way of the development of auto technology, there were some notable exceptions. In the Soviet Union and its satellite states, for example, the government owned the means of production and therefore designed, produced, and sold virtually all the cars in the country. What resulted from this government control? In 1957, the East German government introduced the Trabant, a very poorly made small passenger car with a two-stroke engine. The Trabant went out of production in 1991, following the fall of the Berlin Wall. In its 34 years of existence, only one change had been made to the vehicle. During the 1980s, the original engine was replaced with a West German import, an action made possible by a thawing across the Iron Curtain. Did this mean that the original Trabant embodied the perfect design? Hardly. The same car was in production for 34 years because it was the only model available for people to buy.

America had its own experience with government control of the auto industry: World War II. There were virtually no domestic automobiles produced during the war, because (understandably) everything went to support the war effort. What did we get out of it? In addition to victory, we got the Jeep, over 300,000 of which were produced by Willys-Overland Motors. This example of intervention is notable for being a constitutional exception rather than the unconstitutional rule.

But what we have today is a mixed economy: The role of government and the role of private capital are confused. I would compare our situation to a football game in which the referees change the rules as the game goes along for the purpose of favoring first one side and then the other. This confusion of roles is the source of many of our contemporary problems. One problem began in the 1970s when President Nixon responded to the Arab oil embargo by declaring a program of energy independence. This program, developed under presidents Nixon, Ford, and Carter, consisted of an array of incredibly ill-considered policies. President Carter famously (or infamously) called the fight for energy independence "the moral equivalent of war," a policy the press would come to call by its acronym: MEOW.

Among the ill-conceived policies that have their origin in the 1970s are the Corporate Average Fuel Economy (CAFE) standards. The CAFE standards were enacted in 1975 when President Ford, who vetoed almost everything, declined to veto their implementation. Were the CAFE standards designed to advance automotive technology? Were they designed to provide consumers with better products? Some of those who support the standards say yes, and they make outlandish claims, including the notion that if only Congress and the executive had had the wisdom to raise CAFE standards back in the 1970s, Detroit would not be in the trouble it is in today. Or consider Daniel Becker of the Sierra Club, who has said repeatedly that CAFE standards should be raised to force Detroit to manufacture the kind of vehicles that people want to buy. Extraordinary, isn't it?

Even more extraordinary is that polls seem to indicate the American people support such actions. In 2007, an anti-energy bill enthusiastically passed by Congress and signed by President George W. Bush raised the CAFE standards for passenger cars from the current 27.5 miles per gallon and for light trucks (which includes SUVs) from the current 20.5 miles per gallon to a combined fleet average of 35 miles per gallon by 2020. One poll showed that 91 percent of the American people supported this government interference in consumer choice. How is that possible? Other polling shows why: Over many years the American people have been led to believe that CAFE means that they will be able to buy exactly the same car, with exactly the same performance, in exactly the same size, at exactly the same price, but with much better fuel economy. Who wouldn't support that? But in the real world, the same car with the same performance at the same price will not get twice the mileage. That is not the way the world works.

The lesson here is that raising CAFE standards won't achieve better mileage, but clever people working in Detroit and Tokyo and Bavaria will. Waving the magic wand of CAFE standards will not help us at all in this respect.

By implementing these types of regulations the government is hindering—not helping—the advancement of the auto industry. And, by the way, it is not an exaggeration to say that CAFE kills. When CAFE standards become the most important criterion for new car production, safety goes out the window. The only way a manufacturer can quickly and easily improve the fuel efficiency of an automobile is by making it lighter and smaller. I'll be blunt: Lighter and smaller means that more people will die. The National Research Council has demonstrated the truth of this. It found that in 1993 between 1,300 and 2,600 additional highway fatalities were the result of CAFE standards.

What would Ralph Nader do if he could pin 2,000 additional fatalities on the Ford Motor Company or General Motors each year? You can believe you would be hearing about it. But since the federal government is killing these people, it doesn't matter. I conclude from this that when the government gets involved in the auto industry and auto technology, it does not seek to improve the product or please consumers. It instead has some other purpose that is forcibly superimposed over consumer needs and desires.

In this country, there are two main camps pushing for the active involvement of the federal government in the automobile industry. On the one hand are those who argue that America must reduce its dependence on foreign sources of energy: They believe that CAFE will help us do just that. I believe this is completely fallacious. If we did reduce global demand for petroleum, consider that Saudi Arabia, the lowest cost producer, would be the last country remaining in the market. The first country to go out of the oil business would be the United States. America is a high-cost producer of oil, which means a drop in global demand would tend to drive American producers out. Canada, the largest foreign supplier of oil to the U.S., is also a high-cost producer. In effect, this strategy is a great one, so long as our enemy is Canada!

This line of thinking has roots in the 1970s, and has reappeared in recent years under the banner of what is loosely defined as National Energy Security Conservatives. I think many people who believe this are well-intentioned, and I admire them. But I believe they are wrong. History demonstrates that withdrawing from global markets makes those who do it poorer, and I don't think poverty is going to help our national security.

In the second camp are the environmentalists who are adamant in their belief that higher CAFE standards are needed to save the planet. In other words, higher CAFE standards will help reverse global warming. But if global warming were truly a problem, then the kinds of policies these environmentalists propose, including ever higher CAFE standards and a move from oil to renewable fuels, are completely inadequate. Anyone who truly believes global warming is a serious problem would drop his opposition to nuclear power, for example. Energy rationing, by contrast, only makes us poorer. The only way we are going to transform our economy into a new energy economy is to make ourselves richer. The way to make ourselves richer is by figuring out how to solve environmental problems without demanding a transformation of 85 percent of our energy economy overnight. The magic wand theory won't work. I can only conclude that the global warming scare is not a serious one. Those who seek, by government edict, to force us into ever smaller, less safe, and less commodious cars are not really concerned about global warming. What they do believe is that energy itself is the enemy, because energy gives people power over nature.

In conclusion, the solution to our current problems must begin with an honest and clear assessment of the mixed economy. This can, in turn, help us see clearly the proper role of a limited, constitutional government in a free economy.

Note

1. James D. Johnston, *Driving America: Your Car, Your Government, Your Choice* (Washington: AEI Press, 1997), p. 19.

PAUL J. INGRASSIA

American Cars and American Culture

We have all been told repeatedly by the media in recent years that the reputation of the United States around the world stands—fairly or unfairly—at a low ebb. So why, then, do Sweden and Denmark, among other countries, have avidly active Cadillac clubs—with the most prized model being the 1959 Eldorado, which had the biggest tail fins ever? And why is it almost impossible to find a nation without a Mustang Club? More than 200 such organizations exist worldwide, including clubs in Lithuania, Australia, and the Czech Republic, as well as in America's political and automotive nemeses Russia and Japan.

Clearly, there is a global fascination with American culture—and admiration for America and its culture of freedom—that transcends global geopolitics. And American culture and freedom are uniquely embodied in our nation's automobiles, which have shaped the landscape and reflected the national mood. Indeed, the crossroads between cars and culture is one of the busiest intersections in America.

Amid the thousands of models of cars and trucks sold in the United States over the past century, however, only a handful have defined their time—either by helping to shape American life or by capturing the spirit of an era. Describing America in the 1950s without mentioning tail fins, for instance, would be like describing the New York Yankees of those years without referring to Mickey Mantle. Any account of the rise of the litigious society and of the mistrust of authority that neglects to mention the Chevrolet Corvair is woefully incomplete. The two phases of the 1960s in America—the ebullient first half of the decade and the darker second half—are reflected in the exuberant Ford Mustang and the rebellious Pontiac GTO. The story of the current debate about green cars—and, indeed, a green society—would be impossible to tell without including the surprising success of the Toyota Prius.

My premise here is that certain cars have had a special impact on either defining or shaping the culture of their day. Your first question might well be, "Which was it? Did the cars shape the culture, or did the culture shape the cars?" The answer is yes. It has worked both ways, and will continue to, because cars are so highly visible in our society and so uniquely important in American culture.

The stories behind certain cars reflect many of the fundamental tensions at the core of American culture and life—the conflicts that define who we are as a people. Among these conflicts: big-is-better versus small-is-beautiful; crass and bold versus understated and elegant; practical versus indulgent; self-reliant versus state-reliant; isolationist versus worldly; wholesome versus decadent; rock-and-roll versus Gospel; Saturday night versus Sunday morning.

The Corvair story, for instance, is one of freedom and its attendant risk being laid low by the belief that government should protect citizens from things that could hurt them. This debate rages still (think of motorcycle helmet laws), and creates a core cultural dynamic in America. The popularity of the Accord and of the Beetle reflects the affinity many Americans have for things viewed as "European" or "worldly." By contrast, pickup-truck lovers embrace something quintessentially American—big, muscular, and designed to confer the cowboy virtues of strength and independence upon its owner.

I might add that one could develop a train of thought, and others have, about particular movies, music, works of art, or architecture that have helped shape or reflect American culture. (In 1967, for example, *The Graduate* uniquely captured the alienation and aimlessness of many affluent American young people.) What is different here is that, to my knowledge, no one has taken the approach of looking at trends in modern American culture through the prism of select cars.

I must add that my purpose is not to select the best cars or the worst cars in American history. I will leave it to others to do that—and indeed others have. Good or bad isn't the issue here. The issue is: Has the car had a significant and specific impact on the shape of modern American culture?

I am being highly selective. Many cars are regarded as iconic, such as the Ford Thunderbird and the Ford Taurus, for example. But neither would make my list. Although both were very important when they first appeared (the Thunderbird in the mid-1950s; the Taurus some thirty years later), and both have their aficionados still, I cannot point to a specific cultural impact of either vehicle.

I am including only two cars built before World War II. My premise here, which I concede is subjective, is that the period of major cultural change and upheaval in America occurred in the 60-odd years following the end of WWII.

So which cars are included? Space doesn't permit me to discuss them all here (space— and the need to save a certain element of surprise and suspense for a book I am writing on the subject). But I will discuss several of the included autos in detail. Some of my choices are predictable, and others perhaps not.

I will begin with one that is predictable. It is the car that made America an automotive society, that helped spawn the American middle class, and that is—hands down—the most influential car in American history. There would be a lively debate among historians about which is the second most influential car in our history, but there is no doubt that first place belongs to the Model T Ford.

The Model T was launched in 1908, just over 100 years ago. The intended audience was the common man, and it was priced accordingly. Initially the price tag was $850, which was 25 percent less than that of the competition. It could go anywhere, thanks to Vanadium steel and a flexible frame that could survive the drubbing it received from America's rutted and yet-to-be-developed roadways.

Henry Ford's favorite joke was about the farmer who wanted to be buried in a Model T because it had gotten him out of every hole he had ever been in. The ability to flex with the road, however, did carry a price. One joke of the day is about a Model T owner who named his car the Teddy Roosevelt because it was, after all, the Rough Rider.

Another story, perhaps apocryphal but telling nonetheless, is about the farm wife whose family had a Model T Ford but no indoor plumbing. When asked about her priorities, she replied: "You can't go to town in a bathtub." That says everything about the Model T's appeal.

In the 1920s, the price of the Model T fell as low as $250. But by then America was booming, and to the people entering America's growing and prosperous middle class, transportation as basic—and boring—as the Model T just wasn't enough.

Enter the LaSalle, produced by General Motors. The world's first mass-market designer automobile, it could be labeled America's first Young Urban Professional car (though the term "yuppie" had yet to be invented). It was designed by Harley Earl, the father of automotive styling. Earl had been hired by Alfred Sloan to start GM's "Art and Colour Section," which later became the design department—the auto industry's first design department.

When the *New Yorker* magazine wrote about the LaSalle back in 1927, it said the car was "as refreshing as a Paris smock in a Des Moines ballroom." GM would later use that line in its advertising for the LaSalle, editing out the gratuitous slap at Des Moines!

During the 1930s and the Great Depression, auto sales plunged, of course, and styling took a generally more conservative turn. Then during World War II the nation's auto factories were used to produce military planes and tanks, so production of new cars virtually ceased. The combination of the Depression and oncoming war caused GM to kill the LaSalle brand in 1940, but its influence would be felt in the American cars of the 1950s.

Nineteen fifty-three was a seminal year in America. Dwight D. Eisenhower was in the White House. John F. Kennedy was in the Senate. The Korean War had finally ended. Elvis Presley began his recording career. And Hugh Hefner started *Playboy* magazine. A nation that had endured 25 years of Depression and war was ready to let loose. A *Saturday Evening Post* cover of the time touted a story about "Jack Kennedy, The Senate's Gay Young Bachelor." In the 1950s sense of the wording, of course.

It was also the debut year for the Chevrolet Corvette, a sports car that captured America's postwar spirit. However, the first Corvette was not very good. It had a weak six-cylinder engine, a two-speed automatic transmission, and it leaked like a sieve because of problems with its fiberglass construction. Some owners drilled holes in the floor of their Corvettes so the water would drain out. In fact, the Corvette was so flawed that GM was going to kill the car later in the year. But a low-level engineer came to its rescue.

Zora Arkus-Duntov, a Russian émigré who had fled the Nazis and come to America during World War II, had never lost his youthful fascination with motor vehicles, especially racers. When he saw the Corvette at its introduction at the 1953 Motorama in New York City, he was taken with the car's looks, though not with its engineering. He felt certain he could set things to right, so he sought—and managed to get—a job with GM. He wrote his superiors an iconic memo titled "Thoughts Pertaining to Youth, Hot Rodders and Chevrolet," which made the argument that even if relatively few Corvettes were sold, the car would create excitement for the entire Chevrolet line—especially if those cars were sold to the young hot-rod generation. Thus began the world of youth-targeted marketing, a very significant change in our culture—as any trip to a shopping mall will reveal. And Duntov really did improve the Corvette over the years, step-by-step: a V8 engine in 1955; manual transmission; better suspension and steering. By the late 1960s, it was up to 350 horsepower. The latest—and hottest—Corvette, the ZR1, packs nearly 650 horsepower.

Another symbol of 1950s America is the tail fin. It is ironic that this emblem of peacetime/postwar prosperity was inspired by a war machine—the Lockheed P-38 fighter. Harley Earl had put the first (tiny) fins on the 1948 Cadillac, but it was Chrysler, seeking a design breakthrough, that brought out the big fins in 1955 ... and bigger fins in 1956 and 1957. Chrysler designer Virgil Exner believed that in addition to their good looks, tail fins offered "directional stability enhancement," and so they were promoted as safety devices. But the marketing thrust of the big fin era, "The Forward Look," as it was called, was selling the future: Chrysler's 1957 ads carried the marketing slogan "Suddenly, it's 1960!"

GM responded a few years later. The fins on its 1959 Cadillac Eldorado were the biggest ever: the apogee of tail fins—and, not incidentally, of American postwar exuberance as well. The tail fins on GM's 1959 Caddies are so distinct that today they look like something that George Jetson might have driven, except that the Jetsons' cartoons didn't debut unitl 1962 when tail fins were on the wan. Though they finally disappeared in 1964, tail fins are still prized among car collectors, especially those in Scandinavia, as symbols of America during that period—an America where the sky was the limit, an America that had saved the world from Hitler and was protecting it from communism, an America that offered hope to the world.

But as the tail fin era was closing, the seeds of the American counterculture—then called the beat generation—were stirring. And, speaking of Hitler, it is one of history's great ironies that the Volkswagen Beetle, the Nazi dictator's "People's Car," would evolve into a Hippie icon. The Beetle's original name was the KdF-Wagen, KdF being the abbreviation for *Kraft durch Freude* or "Strength through Joy." That was the name of the Nazi state-sponsored labor movement, and it was bestowed on the Volkswagen by Hitler himself. For some reason, nobody wanted to argue with his choice of a name. But Volkswagen production was halted by World War II. It restarted in the ruins of postwar Germany.

The first VWs came to the United States in 1949, but very few were sold. In the mid-1950s, the company Volkswagen of America was formed. In the late 1950s, it hired the New York ad agency Doyle Dane Bernbach to work on the VW campaign. DDB's clever, irreverent approach propelled the VW "Bug" into automotive history and to immense cultural influence.

One of the first DDB ads for Volkswagen was one of the best, and it set the tone for the next dozen years. It showed a Volkswagen sitting in front of a suburban house on a prosperous street and carried the headline: "What year car do the Jones drive?" The answer, of course, was that you couldn't tell, because all Volkswagens looked the same from year to year. The advertisment's text carried the message that while Detroit was preoccupied with superficial styling changes, Volkswagen was dedicated to quality and functionality. The ad took direct aim at Detroit's annual model change, and indeed at the whole concept of American conspicuous consumption. You might call it downright subversive!

Another VW ad showed a Beetle with a one-word headline: "Lemon." Now to a Detroit executive that was the most foul word in the English language. But the ad told how this particular vehicle had been rejected by one of the company's fussy quality inspectors and sent back to the factory for repair. The punchline: "We pluck the lemons, so you get the plums."

The hip, irreverent advertising helped make the Beetle a totem of the growing U.S. counterculture movement of the 1960s and early 1970s. That was especially true of the VW microbus. One ad showed an empty microbus, with its doors open, and the headline: "Do you have the right kind of wife for it?" The headline sounds terribly sexist today, but the text described an independent woman worried about world peace, one who would choose not to buy new household furniture so that she and her husband could take a trip to Europe instead. The microbus's counter-status was cemented in 1995 when Jerry Garcia, leader of the Grateful Dead rock band, passed away at age 53. Volkswagen ran a full-page ad in *Rolling Stone* magazine that showed a sparsely sketched microbus facing straight ahead, shedding a single tear from one of its headlights. The caption said simply: "Jerry Garcia: 1942 1995." Very poignant, indeed.

Another of America's most influential automobiles, also built in the 1960s, was GM's Chevrolet Corvair. It was one of the Big Three's first generation of compact cars, and it debuted in 1960. Mechanically the Corvair was similar to the VW Beetle, with a rear-mounted, air-cooled engine mounted directly over the drive wheels, instead of the conventional front-mounted water-cooled engine with the drive wheels at the opposite end of the car. The Corvair was lightweight and fuel-efficient, getting nearly 30 miles a gallon on the highway—the Prius of its day, in many ways. Ed Cole, a brilliant engineer who ran Chevrolet, and who later became GM's president, headed the car's development effort. Unlike the Beetle of that day, the Corvair was available in a variety of body styles—two-door coupes, four-door coupes, station wagons, and even a camper van.

But the Corvair had a problem. The concentration of weight in the rear of the car often caused a "spin-out" effect when it took corners, and there were a growing number of accidents involving serious injuries that stemmed from Corvairs spinning out around curves or corners. One man who noticed was a young lawyer named Ralph Nader, and he wrote a book called *Unsafe at Any Speed*, published in 1965. The book didn't generate much attention and sales were sparse—until GM shot itself in the foot. The news broke that General Motors had hired a private detective to spy on the young Mr. Nader. Congressional hearings were convened. GM's president, Jim Roche, ended up publicly apologizing to Mr. Nader before a congressional committee—and also before the network television cameras. The uproar that followed propelled *Unsafe at Any Speed* onto the best-seller list, and it propelled Ralph Nader to national and international prominence.

The Nader effect was pervasive. Within 18 months of those hearings, Congress passed five major new laws regulating industry—and not just the auto industry, but natural gas, meat-packing, and more. Nader's book, and the response to it, spawned both the American consumer movement and an explosion in product liability litigation. There is a direct line of descent, in fact, from the Corvair litigation in the early 1960s to another famous "defective product" case—the one in which an elderly woman successfully sued McDonalds for getting badly burned with hot coffee. That verdict was reversed on appeal, after becoming a national symbol, rightly or wrongly, for litigation spinning out of control.

Beyond all this, Ralph Nader might even be responsible for George W. Bush becoming president in 2000. Nader was a presidential candidate that year as well, and he received 98,000 votes in Florida. Bush won the state by only 1,800 votes over Al Gore, and virtually all the Nader votes would have gone to Gore had Nader not been in the race. And this was 40 years after the Corvair first appeared on American roads. Talk about a long-term cultural legacy. This is why the Corvair gets my vote for the second most influential car in American history, after, of course, the Model T.

Another vehicle that had a distinct impact on American culture was the Chrysler minivan, introduced in 1984. Not only did it revolutionize family transportation, it also spawned a truck boom in America that lasted a quarter century. After the minivan boomed in popularity, sport-utility vehicles also emerged as mainstream automobiles. They uniquely captured the spirit of the outdoor-recreation boom that created the atmosphere in which companies like Patagonia, North Face, and Timberland thrived by catering to Americans who wanted to rough it—but be comfortable in the process.

Pickup trucks, which had been around for decades, mostly driven by ranchers, farmers, and contractors, followed SUVs into the mainstream. In the 1990s, they started being driven by a new breed of suburban cowboys—in places like Naperville, Illinois, and Plano, Texas—by people who didn't really need a truck, and who hauled plywood not to make a living but instead, you know, to show off. The pickup-truck boom was all about cowboys, country music, and red-state America, forces that dominated national politics during the first years of the twenty-first century, much to the consternation of *The New York Times*. Pickups also basically saved Ford Motor Company, which dominated that market segment for about 15 years, beginning in the early 1990s.

Every reaction has an equal and opposite reaction, in cars as well as in physics. So I will end this discussion by turning from trucks to cite the cultural influence of the Pious, I mean the Prius, which is made by Toyota and is the first commercially successful gas-hybrid electric vehicle. The Prius is a great car, even if the attitude of the people who drive it can be somewhat insufferable.

But the Prius isn't a panacea. Nor are hybrids the only solution to automotive environmental issues. In fact, some of the modern clean-burning diesel engines from Europe provide almost all of the environmental benefits that the Prius does. But what Hollywood star wants to be seen driving a diesel as opposed to a "green" hybrid vehicle? Make no mistake about it, however. The Prius has redefined the discussion of what personal transportation—that is, automotive transportation—should be in the twenty-first century. And therefore it has exerted an enormous influence on modern American culture.

Cars tap deep emotions and memories in people, especially in Americans. The recent government bailouts and bankruptcies of GM and Chrysler cost only about one-seventh the amount that taxpayers spent to bail out Wall Street and America's banks. But it is cars, not banks, that are celebrated in music, movies, and books. In 1963 the Beach Boys sang "Little Deuce Coupe," not "Little Deuce Coupon."

And three years later, Wilson Pickett's hit song was "Mustang Sally," not "Mustang Sallie Mae."

Cars have helped shape our culture. They helped produce suburbs, fast-food restaurants, national hotel chains, and the interstate highway sytem. You might call these things the 4H Club: housing, hamburgers, hotels, and highways.

And a few special automobiles have had an especially pervasive and powerful impact on the way Americans live.

LUDWIG VON MISES

EXCERPTS FROM

ECONOMIC POLICY:
THOUGHTS FOR TODAY AND TOMORROW

Lecture 2: Socialism

I am here in Buenos Aires as a guest of the Centro de Difusión Economía Libre.* What is *economía libre*? What does this system of economic freedom mean? The answer is simple: it is the market economy, it is the system in which the cooperation of individuals in the social division of labor is achieved by the market. This market is not a place; it is a process, it is the way in which, by selling and buying, by producing and consuming, the individuals contribute to the total workings of society.

In dealing with this system of economic organization—the market economy—we employ the term "economic freedom." Very often, people misunderstand what it means, believing that economic freedom is something quite apart from other freedoms, and that these other freedom—which they hold to be more important—can be preserved even in the absence of economic freedom. The meaning of economic freedom is this: that the individual is in a position to choose the way in which he wants to integrate himself into the totality of society. The individual is able to choose his career, he is free to do what he wants to do.

---

*Later the Centro de Estudios sobre la Libertad

Reprinted with permission from Ludwig von Mises, *Economic Policy: Thoughts for Today and Tomorrow*, 3rd ed. (Auburn, AL: Ludwig von Mises Institute, 2006), pp. 17–36, 37–54. http://mises.org.

This is of course not meant in any sense which so many people attach to the word freedom today; it is meant rather in the sense that, through economic freedom, man is freed from natural conditions. In nature, there is nothing that can be termed freedom, there is only the regularity of the laws of nature, which man must obey if he wants to attain something.

In using the term freedom as applied to human beings, we think only of freedom *within society*. Yet, today, social freedoms are considered by many people to be independent of one another. Those who call themselves "liberals" today are asking for policies which are precisely the opposite of those policies which the liberals of the nineteenth century advocated in their liberal programs. The so-called liberals of today have the very popular idea that freedom of speech, of thought, of the press, freedom of religion, freedom from imprisonment without trial—that all these freedoms can be preserved in the absence of what is called economic freedom. They do not realize that, in a system where there is no market, where the government directs everything, all those other freedoms are illusory, even if they are made into laws and written up in constitutions.

Let us take one freedom, the freedom of the press. If the government owns all the printing presses, it will determine what is to be printed and what is not to be printed. And if the government owns all the printing presses and determines what shall or shall not be printed, then the possibility of printing any kind of opposing arguments against the ideas of the government becomes practically nonexistent. Freedom of the press disappears. And it is the same with all the other freedoms.

In a market economy, the individual has the freedom to choose whatever career he wishes to pursue, to choose his own way of integrating himself into society. But in a socialist system, that is not so: his career is decided by decree of the government. The government can order people whom it dislikes, whom it does not want to live in certain regions, to move into other regions and to other places. And the government is always in a position to justify and to explain such procedure by declaring that the governmental plan requires the presence of this eminent citizen five thousand miles away from the place in which he could be disagreeable to those in power.

It is true that the freedom a man may have in a market economy is not a perfect freedom from the metaphysical point of view. But there is no such thing as perfect freedom. Freedom means something only within the framework of society. The eighteenth-century authors of "natural law"—above all, Jean Jacques Rousseau—believed that once, in the remote past, men enjoyed something called "natural" freedom. But in that remote age, individuals were not free, they were at the mercy of everyone who was stronger than they were. The famous words of Rousseau: "Man is born free and everywhere he is in chains" may sound good, but man is in fact *not* born free. Man is born a very weak suckling. Without the protection of his parents, without the protection given to his parents by society, he would not be able to preserve his life.

Freedom in society means that a man depends as much upon other people as other people depend upon him. Society under the market economy, under the conditions of "economía libre," means a state of affairs in which everybody serves his fellow citizens and is served by them in return. People believe that there are in the market economy bosses who are independent of the good will and support of other people. They believe that the captains of industry, the businessmen, the entrepreneurs are the real bosses in the economic system. But this is an illusion. The real bosses in the economic system are the consumers. And if the consumers stop patronizing a branch of business, these businessmen are either forced to abandon their eminent position in the economic system or to adjust their actions to the wishes and to the orders of the consumers.

One of the best-known propagators of communism was Lady Passfield, under her maiden name Beatrice Potter, and well-known also through her husband Sidney Webb. This lady was the daughter of a wealthy businessman and, when she was a young adult, she served as her father's secretary. In her memoirs she writes: "In the business of my father everybody had to obey the orders issued by my father, the boss. He alone had to give orders, but to him nobody gave any orders." This is a very short-sighted view. Orders *were* given to her father by the consumers, by the buyers. Unfortunately, she could not see *these* orders; she could not see what goes on in a market economy, because she was interested only in the orders given within her father's office or his factory.

In all economic problems, we must bear in mind the words of the great French economist Frédéric Bastiat, who titled one of his brilliant essays: "*Ce qu'on voit et ce qu'on ne voit pas*" ("That which is seen and that which is not seen"). In order to comprehend the operation of an economic system, we must deal not only with the things that can be seen, but we also have to give our attention to the things which cannot be perceived directly. For instance, an order issued by a boss to an office boy can be heard by everybody who is present in the room. What cannot be heard are the orders given to the boss by his customers.

The fact is that, under the capitalistic system, the ultimate bosses are the consumers. The sovereign is not the state, it is the people. And the proof that they are the sovereign is borne out by the fact that they have *the right to be foolish*. This is the privilege of the sovereign. He has the right to make mistakes, no one can prevent him from making them, but of course he has to pay for his mistakes. If we say the consumer is supreme or that the consumer is sovereign, we do not say that the consumer is free from faults, that the consumer is a man who always knows what would be best for him. The consumers very often buy things or consume things they ought not to buy or ought not to consume.

But the notion that a capitalist form of government can prevent people from hurting themselves by controlling their consumption is false. The idea of government as a paternal authority, as a guardian for everybody, is the idea of those who favor socialism. In the United States some years ago, the government tried what was called "a noble experiment." This noble experiment was a law making it illegal to buy or sell intoxicating beverages. It is certainly true that many people drink too much brandy and whiskey, and that they may hurt themselves by doing so. Some authorities in the United States are even opposed to smoking. Certainly there are many people who smoke too much and who smoke in spite of the fact that it would be better for them not to smoke. This raises a question which goes far beyond economic discussion: it shows what freedom really means.

Granted, that it is good to keep people from hurting themselves by drinking or smoking too much. But once you have admitted this, other people will say: Is the body everything? Is not the mind of man much more important? Is not the mind of man the real human endowment, the real human quality? If you give the government the right to determine the consumption of the human body, to determine whether one should smoke or not smoke, drink or not drink, there is no good reply you can give to people who say: "More important than the body is the mind and the soul, and man hurts himself much more by reading bad books, by listening to bad music and looking at bad movies. Therefore it is the duty of the government to prevent people from committing these faults."

And, as you know, for many hundreds of years governments and authorities believed that this really *was* their duty. Nor did this happen in far distant ages only; not long ago, there was a government in Germany that considered it a governmental duty to distinguish between good and bad paintings—which of course meant good and bad from the point of view of a man who, in his youth, had failed the entrance examination at the Academy of Art in Vienna; good and bad from the point of view of a picture-postcard painter, Adolf Hitler. And it became illegal for people to utter other views about art and paintings than his, the Supreme Führer's.

Once you begin to admit that it is the duty of the government to control your consumption of alcohol, what can you reply to those who say the control of books and ideas is much more important?

Freedom really means *the freedom to make mistakes*. This we have to realize. We may be highly critical with regard to the way in which our fellow citizens are spending their money and living their lives. We may believe that what they are doing is absolutely foolish and bad, but in a free society, there are many ways for people to air their opinions on how their fellow citizens should change their ways of life. They can write books; they can write articles; they can make speeches; they can even preach at street corners if they want—and they do this in many countries. But they must *not* try to police other people in order to prevent them from doing certain things simply because they themselves do not want these other people to have the freedom to do it.

This is the difference between slavery and freedom. The slave must do what his superior orders him to do, but the free citizen—and this is what freedom means—is in a position to choose his own way of life. Certainly this capitalistic system can be abused, and is abused, by some people. It is certainly possible to do things which ought not to be done. But if these things are approved by a majority of the people, a disapproving person always has a way to attempt to change the minds of his fellow citizens. He can try to persuade them, to convince them, but he may not try to force them by the use of power, of governmental police power.

In the market economy, everyone serves his fellow citizens by serving himself. This is what the liberal authors of the eighteenth century had in mind when they spoke of the harmony of the rightly understood interests of all groups and of all individuals of the population. And it was this doctrine of the harmony of interests which the socialists opposed. They spoke of an "irreconcilable conflict of interests" between various groups.

What does this mean? When Karl Marx—in the first chapter of the *Communist Manifesto*, that small pamphlet which inaugurated his socialist movement—claimed that there was an irreconcilable conflict between classes, he could not illustrate his thesis by any examples other than those drawn from the conditions of precapitalistic society. In precapitalistic ages, society was divided into hereditary status groups, which in India are called "castes." In a status society a man was not, for example, born a Frenchman; he was born as a member of the French aristocracy or of the French bourgeoisie or of the French peasantry. In the greater part of the Middle Ages, he was simply a serf. And serfdom, in France, did not disappear completely until after the American Revolution. In other parts of Europe it disappeared even later.

But the worst form in which serfdom existed—and continued to exist even after the abolition of slavery—was in the British colonies abroad. The individual inherited his status from his parents, and he retained it throughout his life. He transferred it to his children. Every group had privileges and disadvantages. The highest groups had only privileges, the lowest groups only disadvantages. And there was no way a man could rid himself of the legal disadvantages placed upon him by his status other than by fighting a political struggle against the other classes. Under such conditions, you could say that there was an "irreconcilable conflict of interests between the slave owners and the slaves," because what the slaves wanted was to be rid of their slavery, of their quality of being slaves. This meant a loss, however, for the owners. Therefore, there is no question that there had to be this irreconcilable conflict of interests between the members of the various classes.

One must not forget that in those ages—in which the status societies were predominant in Europe, as well as in the colonies which the Europeans later founded in America—people did not consider themselves to be connected in any special way with the other classes of their own nation; they felt much more at one with the members of their own class in other countries. A French aristocrat did not look upon lower class Frenchmen as his fellow citizens; they were the "rabble," which he did not like. He regarded only the aristocrats of other countries—those of Italy, England, and Germany, for instance, as his equals.

The most visible effect of this state of affairs was the fact that the aristocrats all over Europe used the same language. And this language was French, a language which was not understood, outside France, by other groups of the population. The middle classes—the bourgeoisie—had their own language, while the lower classes—the peasantry—used local dialects which very often were not understood by other groups of the population. The same was true with regard to the way people dressed. When you travelled in 1750 from one country to another, you found that the upper classes, the aristocrats, were usually dressed in the same way all over Europe, and you found that the lower classes dressed differently. When you met someone in the street, you could see immediately—from the way he dressed—to which class, to which status he belonged.

It is difficult to imagine how different these conditions were from present-day conditions. When I come from the United States to Argentina and I see a man on the street, I cannot know what his status is. I only assume that he is a citizen of Argentina and that he is not a member of some legally restricted group. This is one thing that capitalism has brought about. Of course, there are also differences within capitalism. There are differences in wealth, differences which Marxians mistakenly consider to be equivalent to the old differences that existed between men in the status society.

The differences within a capitalist society are not the same as those in a socialist society. In the Middle Ages—and in many countries even much later—a family could be an aristocrat family and possess great wealth, it could be a family of dukes for hundreds and hundreds of years, whatever its qualities, its talents, its character or morals. But, under modern capitalistic conditions, there is what has been technically described by sociologists as "social mobility." The operating principle of this social mobility, according to the Italian sociologist and economist Vilfredo Pareto, is "la circulation des élites" ("the circulation of the elites"). This means that there are always people who are at the top of the social ladder, who are wealthy, who are politically important, but these people—these elites—are continually changing.

This is perfectly true in a capitalist society. It was *not* true for a precapitalistic status society. The families who were considered the great aristocratic families of Europe are still the same families today or, let us say, they are the descendants of families that were foremost in Europe, 800 or 1000 or more years ago. The Capetians of Bourbon—who for a very long time ruled here in Argentina—were a royal house as early as the tenth century. These kings ruled the territory which is known now as the Ile-de-France, extending their reign from generation to generation. But in a capitalist society, there is continuous mobility—poor people becoming rich and the descendants of those rich people losing their wealth and becoming poor.

Today I saw in a bookshop in one of the central streets of Buenos Aires the biography of a businessman who was so eminent, so important, so characteristic of big business in the nineteenth century in Europe that, even in this country, far away from Europe, the bookshop carried copies of his biography. I happen to know the grandson of this man. He has the same name his grandfather had, and he still has a right to wear the title of nobility which his grandfather—who started as a blacksmith—had received eighty years ago. Today this grandson is a poor photographer in New York City.

Other people, who were poor at the time this photographer's grandfather became one of Europe's biggest industrialists, are today captains of industry. Everyone is free to change his status. That is the difference between the status system and the capitalist system of economic freedom, in which everyone has only himself to blame if he does not reach the position he wants to reach.

The most famous industrialist of the twentieth century up to now is Henry Ford. He started with a few hundred dollars which he had borrowed from his friends, and within a very short time he developed one of the most important big business firms of the world. And one can discover hundreds of such cases every day.

Every day, the *New York Times* prints long notices of people who have died. If you read these biographies, you may come across the name of an eminent businessman, who started out as a seller of newspapers at street corners in New York. Or he started as an office boy, and at his death he was the president of the same banking firm where he started on the lowest rung of the ladder. Of course, not all people can attain these positions. Not all people *want* to attain them. There are people who are more interested in other problems and, for these people, other ways are open today which were not open in the days of feudal society, in the ages of the status society.

The socialist system, however, *forbids* this fundamental freedom to choose one's own career. Under socialist conditions, there is only one economic authority, and it has the right to determine all matters concerning production.

One of the characteristic features of our day is that people use many names for the same thing. One synonym for socialism and communism is "planning." If people speak of "planning" they mean, of course, *central* planning, which means *one plan made by the government*—one plan that prevents planning by anyone except the government.

A British lady, who also is a member of the Upper House, wrote a book entitled *Plan or No Plan*, a book which was quite popular around the world. What does the title of her book mean? When she says "plan," she means only the type of plan envisioned by Lenin and Stalin and their successors, the type which governs all the activities of all the people of a nation. Thus, this lady means a central plan which excludes all the personal plans that individuals may have. Her title *Plan or No Plan* is therefore an illusion, a deception; the alternative is not a central plan or no plan, it is *the total plan* of a central governmental authority or *freedom* for individuals to make their own plans, to do their own planning. The individual plans his life, every day, changing his daily plans whenever he will.

The free man plans daily for his needs; he says, for example: "Yesterday I planned to work all my life in Córdoba." Now he learns about better conditions in Buenos Aires and changes his plans, saying: "Instead of working in Córdoba, I want to go to Buenos Aires." And that is what freedom means. It may be that he is mistaken, it may be that his going to Buenos Aires will turn out to have been a mistake.

Conditions may have been better for him in Córdoba, but he himself made his plans.

Under government planning, he is like a soldier in an army. The soldier in the army does not have the right to choose his garrison, to choose the place where he will serve. He has to obey orders. And the socialist system—as Karl Marx, Lenin, and all socialist leaders knew and admitted—is the transfer of army rule to the whole production system. Marx spoke of "industrial armies," and Lenin called for "the organization of everything—the postoffice, the factory, and other industries, according to the model of the army."

Therefore, in the socialist system everything depends on the wisdom, the talents, and the gifts of those people who form the supreme authority. That which the supreme dictator—or his committee—does *not* know, is not taken into account. But the knowledge which mankind has accumulated in its long history is not acquired by everyone; we have accumulated such an enormous amount of scientific and technical knowledge over the centuries that it is humanly impossible for one individual to know all these things, even though he be a most gifted man.

And people are different, they are unequal. They always will be. There are some people who are more gifted in one subject and less in another one. And there are people who have the gift to find new paths, to change the trend of knowledge. In capitalist societies, technological progress and economic progress are gained through such people. If a man has an idea, he will try to find a few people who are clever enough to realize the value of his idea. Some capitalists, who dare to look into the future, who realize the possible consequences of such an idea, will start to put it to work. Other people, at first, may say: "They are fools"; but they will stop saying so when they discover that this enterprise, which they called foolish, is flourishing, and that people are happy to buy its products.

Under the Marxian system, on the other hand, the supreme government body must first be convinced of the value of such an idea before it can be pursued and developed. This can be a very difficult thing to do, for only the group of people at the head—or the supreme dictator himself—has the power to make decisions. And if these people—because of laziness or old age, or because they are not very bright and learned—are unable to grasp the importance of the new idea, then the new project will not be undertaken.

We can think of examples from military history. Napoleon was certainly a genius in military affairs; he had one serious problem, however, and his inability to solve that problem culminated, finally, in his defeat and exile to the loneliness of St. Helena. Napoleon's problem was: "How to conquer England?" In order to do that, he needed a navy to cross the English Channel, and there were people who told him they had a way to accomplish that crossing, people who—in an age of sailing ships—had come up with the new idea of steam ships. But Napoleon did not understand their proposal.

Then there was Germany's *Generalstab*, the famous German general staff. Before the First World War, it was universally considered to be unsurpassed in military wisdom. A similar reputation was held by the staff of General Foch in France. But neither the Germans nor the French—who, under the leadership of General Foch, later defeated the Germans—realized the importance of aviation for military purposes. The German general staff said: "Aviation is merely for pleasure, flying is good for idle people. From a military point of view, only the Zeppelins are important" and the French general staff was of the same opinion.

Later, during the period between World War I and World War II, there was a general in the United States who was convinced that aviation would be very important in the next war. But all other experts in the United States were against him. He could not convince them. If you have to convince a group of people who are not directly dependent on the solution of a problem, you will never succeed. This is true also of noneconomic problems.

There have been painters, poets, writers, composers, who complained that the public did not acknowledge their work and caused them to remain poor. The public may certainly have had poor judgment, but when these artists said: "The government ought to support great artists, painters, and writers," they were very much in the wrong. Whom should the government entrust with the task of deciding whether a newcomer is really a great painter or not? It would have to rely on the judgment of the critics, and the professors of the history of art who are always looking back into the past yet who very rarely have shown the talent to discover new genius. This is the great difference between a system of "planning" and a system in which everyone can plan and act for himself.

It is true, of course, that great painters and great writers have often had to endure great hardships. They might have succeeded in their art, but not always in getting money. Van Gogh was certainly a great painter. He had to suffer unbearable hardship and, finally, when he was thirty-seven years old, he committed suicide. In all his life he sold only *one painting* and the buyer of it was his cousin. Apart from this one sale, he lived from the money of his brother, who was not an artist nor a painter. But van Gogh's brother understood a painter's needs. Today you cannot buy a van Gogh for less than hundred or two hundred thousand dollars.

Under a socialist system, van Gogh's fate might have been different. Some government official would have asked some well-known painters (whom van Gogh certainly would not have regarded as artists at all) whether this young man, half or completely crazy, was really a painter worthy to be supported. And they without a doubt, would have answered: "No, he is not a painter; he is not an artist; he is just a man who wastes paint;" and they would have sent him into a milk factory or into a home for the insane. Therefore all this enthusiasm in favor of socialism by the rising generation of painters, poets, musicians, journalists, actors, is based on an *illusion*. I mention this because these groups are among the most fanatical supporters of the socialist idea.

When it comes to choosing between socialism and capitalism as an economic system, the problem is somewhat different. The authors of socialism never suspected that modern industry, and all the operations of modern business, are based on calculation. Engineers are by no means the only ones who make plans on the basis of calculations, businessmen also must do so. And businessmen's calculations are all based on the fact that, in the market economy, the money prices of goods inform not only the consumer, they also provide vital information to businessmen about the factors of production, the main function of the market being not merely to determine the cost of the *last* part of the process of production and transfer of goods to the hands of the consumer, but the cost of those steps leading up to it. The whole market system is bound up with the fact that there is a mentally calculated division of labor between the various businessmen who vie with each other in bidding for the factors of production—the raw materials, the machines, the instruments—and for the human factor of production, the wages paid to labor. This sort of calculation by the businessman cannot be accomplished in the absence of prices supplied by the market.

At the very instant you abolish the market—which is what the socialists would like to do—you render useless all the computations and calculations of the engineers and technologists. The technologists can give you a great number of projects which, from the point of view of the natural sciences, are equally feasible, but it takes the market-based *calculations* of the businessman to make clear which of those projects is the most advantageous, from the *economic* point of view.

The problem with which I am dealing here is the fundamental issue of capitalistic economic calculation as opposed to socialism. The fact is that economic calculation, and therefore all technological planning, is possible only if there are money prices, not only for consumer goods but also for the factors of production. This means there has to be a market for raw materials, for all half-finished goods, for all tools and machines, and for all kinds of human labor and human services.

When this fact was discovered, the socialists did not know how to respond. For 150 years they had said: "All the evils in the world come from the fact that there are markets and market prices. We want to abolish the market and with it, of course, the market economy, and substitute for it a system without prices and without markets." They wanted to abolish what Marx called the "commodity character" of commodities and of labor.

When faced with this new problem, the authors of socialism, having no answer, finally said: "We will not abolish the market altogether; we will pretend that a market exists; we will play market like children who play school." But everyone knows that when children *play* school, they do not learn anything. It is just an exercise, a game, and you can "play" at many things.

This is a very difficult and complicated problem and in order to deal with it in full one needs a little more time than I have here. I have explained it in detail in my writings. In six lectures I cannot enter into an analysis of all its aspects. Therefore, I want to advise you, if you are interested in the fundamental problem of the impossibility of calculation and planning under socialism, read my book *Human Action*, which is available in an excellent Spanish translation.

But read other books, too, like the book of the Norwegian economist Trygve Hoff, who wrote on economic calculation. And if you do not want to be one-sided, I recommend that you read the highly-regarded socialist book on this subject by the eminent Polish economist Oskar Lange, who at one time was a professor at an American university, then became a Polish ambassador, and later returned to Poland.

You will probably ask me: "What about Russia? How do the Russians handle this question?" This changes the problem. The Russians operate their socialistic system within a world in which there are prices for all the factors of production, for all raw materials, for everything. They can therefore employ, for their planning, the *foreign* prices of the world market. And because there are certain differences between conditions in Russia and those in United States, the result is very often that the Russians consider something to be justified and advisable—from their economic point of view—that the Americans would not consider economically justifiable at all.

The "Soviet experiment," as it was called, does not prove anything. It does not tell us anything about the fundamental problem of socialism, the problem of calculation. But are we entitled to speak of it as an experiment? I do not believe there is such a thing as a scientific experiment in the field of human action and economics. You cannot make laboratory experiments in the field of human action because a scientific experiment requires that you do the same thing under various conditions, or that you maintain the same conditions, changing perhaps only one factor. For instance, if you inject into a cancerous animal some experimental medication, the result may be that the cancer will disappear. You can test this with various animals of the same kind which suffer from the same malignancy. If you treat some of them with the new method and do not treat the rest, then you can compare the result. You cannot do this within the field of human action. There are no laboratory experiments in human action.

The so-called Soviet "experiment" merely shows that the standard of living is incomparably lower in Soviet Russia than it is in the country that is considered, by the whole world, as the paragon of capitalism: the United States.

Of course, if you tell this to a socialist, he will say: "Things are wonderful in Russia." And you tell him: "They may be wonderful, but the average standard of living is much lower." Then he will answer: "Yes, but remember how terrible it was for the Russians under the tsars and how terrible a war we had to fight."

I do not want to enter into discussion of whether this is or is not a correct explanation, but if you deny that the conditions are the same, you deny that it was an experiment. You must then say this (which would be much more correct): "Socialism in Russia has not brought about an improvement in the conditions of the average man which can be compared with the improvement of conditions, during the same period, in the United States."

In the United States you hear of something new, of some improvement, almost every week. These are improvements that business has generated, because thousands and thousands of business people are trying day and night to find some new product which satisfies the consumer better or is less expensive to produce, or better *and* less expensive than the existing products. They do not do this out of altruism, they do it because they want to make money. And the effect is that you have an improvement in the standard of living in the United States which is almost miraculous, when compared with the conditions that existed fifty or a hundred years ago. But in Soviet Russia, where you do not have such a system, you do not have a comparable improvement. So those people who tell us that we ought to adopt the Soviet system are badly mistaken.

There is something else that should be mentioned. The American consumer, the individual, is both a buyer and a boss. When you leave a store in America, you may find a sign saying: "Thank you for your patronage. Please come again." But when you go into a shop in a totalitarian country—be it in present-day Russia, or in Germany as it was under the regime of Hitler—the shopkeeper tells you: "You have to be thankful to the great leader for giving you this."

In socialist countries, it is not the seller who has to be grateful, it is the buyer. The citizen is *not* the boss; the boss is the Central Committee, the Central Office. Those socialist committees and leaders and dictators are supreme, and the people simply have to obey them.

Lecture 3: Interventionism

A famous, very often quoted phrase says: "That government is best, which governs least." I do not believe this to be a correct description of the functions of a good government. Government ought to do all the things for which it is needed and for which it was established. Government ought to protect the individuals within the country against the violent and fraudulent attacks of gangsters, and it should defend the country against foreign enemies. These are the functions of government within a free system, within the system of the market economy.

Under socialism, of course, the government is totalitarian, and there is nothing outside its sphere and its jurisdiction. But in the market economy the main task of the government is to protect the smooth functioning of the market economy against fraud or violence from within and from outside the country.

People who do not agree with this definition of the functions of government may say: "This man hates the government." Nothing could be farther from the truth. If I should say that gasoline is a very useful liquid, useful for many purposes, but that I would nevertheless not drink gasoline because I think that would not be the right use for it, I am not an enemy of gasoline, and I do not hate gasoline. I only say that gasoline is very useful for certain purposes, but not fit for other purposes. If I say it is the government's duty to arrest murderers and other criminals, but not its duty to run the railroads or to spend money for useless things, then I do not hate the government by declaring that it is fit to do certain things but not fit to do other things.

It has been said that under present-day conditions we no longer have a free market economy. Under present-day conditions we have something called the "mixed economy." And for evidence of our "mixed economy," people point to the many enterprises which are operated and owned by the government. The economy is mixed, people say, because there are, in many countries, certain institutions—like the telephone, telegraph, and railroads—which are owned and operated by the government.

That some of these institutions and enterprises are operated by the government is certainly true. But this fact alone does *not* change the character of our economic system. It does not even mean there is a "little socialism" within the otherwise nonsocialist, free market economy. For the government, in operating these enterprises, is subject to the supremacy of the market, which means it is subject to the supremacy of the consumers. The government—if it operates, let us say, post offices or railroads—has to hire people who have to work in these enterprises. It also has to buy the raw materials and other things that are needed for the conduct of these enterprises. And on the other hand, it "sells" these services or commodities to the public. Yet, even though it operates these institutions using the methods of the free economic system, the result, as a rule, is a deficit. The government, however, is in a position to finance such a deficit—at least the members of the government and of the ruling party believe so.

It is certainly different for an individual. The individual's power to operate something with a deficit is very limited. If the deficit is not very soon eliminated, and if the enterprise does not become profitable (or at least show that no further deficit losses are being incurred), the individual goes bankrupt and the enterprise must come to an end.

But for the government, conditions are different. The government can run at a deficit, because it has the power to *tax* people. And if the taxpayers are prepared to pay higher taxes in order to make it possible for the government to operate an enterprise at a loss—that is, in a less efficient way than it would be done by a private institution—and if the public will accept this loss, then of course the enterprise will continue.

In recent years, governments have increased the number of nationalized institutions and enterprises in most countries to such an extent that the deficits have grown far beyond the amount that could be collected in taxes from the citizens. What happens then is not the subject of today's lecture. It is inflation, and I shall deal with that tomorrow. I mentioned this only because the mixed economy must not be confused with the problem of *interventionism*, about which I want to talk tonight.

What is interventionism? Interventionism means that the government does not restrict its activity to the preservation of order, or—as people used to say a hundred years ago—to "the production of security." Interventionism means that the government wants to do more. It wants to interfere with market phenomena.

If one objects and says the government should not interfere with business, people very often answer: "But the government necessarily always interferes. If there are policemen on the street, the government interferes. It interferes with a robber looting a shop or it prevents a man from stealing a car." But when dealing with interventionism and defining what is meant by interventionism, we are speaking about government interference with the market. (That the government and the police are expected to protect the citizens, which includes businessmen, and of course their employees, against attacks on the part of domestic or foreign gangsters, is in fact a normal, necessary expectation of any government. Such protection is not an intervention, for the government's only legitimate function is, precisely, to produce security.)

What we have in mind when we talk about interventionism is the government's desire to do *more* than prevent assaults and fraud. Interventionism means that the government not only fails to protect the smooth functioning of the market economy, but that it interferes with the various market phenomena; it interferes with prices, with wage rates, interest rates, and profits.

The government wants to interfere in order to force businessmen to conduct their affairs in a different way than they would have chosen if they had obeyed only the consumers. Thus, all the measures of interventionism by the government are directed toward restricting the supremacy of consumers. The government wants to arrogate to itself the power, or at least a part of the power, which, in the free market economy, is in the hands of the consumers.

Let us consider one example of interventionism, very popular in many countries and tried again and again by many governments, especially in times of inflation. I refer to price control.

Governments usually resort to price control when they have inflated the money supply and people have begun to complain about the resulting rise in prices. There are many famous historical examples of price control methods that failed, but I shall refer to only two of them because, in both these cases, the governments were really very energetic in enforcing or trying to enforce their price controls.

The first famous example is the case of the Roman Emperor Diocletian, very well-known as the last of those Roman emperors who persecuted the Christians. The Roman emperor in the second part of the third century had only one financial method, and this was currency debasement. In those primitive ages, before the invention of the printing press, even inflation was, let us say, primitive. It involved debasement of the coinage, especially the silver. The government mixed more and more copper into the silver until the color of the silver coins was changed and the weight was reduced considerably. The result of this coinage debasement and the associated increase in the quantity of money was an increase in prices, followed by an edict to control prices. And Roman emperors were not very mild when they enforced a law; they did not consider death too mild a punishment for a man who had asked for a higher price. They enforced price control, but they failed to maintain the society. The result was the disintegration of the Roman Empire and the system of the division of labor.

Then, 1500 years later, the same currency debasement took place during the French Revolution. But this time a different method was used. The technology for producing money was considerably improved. It was no longer necessary for the French to resort to debasement of the coinage: they had the printing press. And the printing press was very efficient. Again, the result was an unprecedented rise in prices. But in the French Revolution maximum prices were not enforced by the same method of capital punishment which the Emperor Diocletian had used. There had also been an improvement in the technique of killing citizens. You all remember the famous Doctor J. I. Guillotin (1738-1814), who advocated the use of the guillotine. Despite the guillotine the French also failed with their laws of maximum prices. When Robespierre himself was carted off to the guillotine the people shouted, "There goes the dirty Maximum."

I wanted to mention this, because people often say: "What is needed in order to make price control effective and efficient is merely more brutality and more energy." Now certainly, Diocletian was very brutal, and so was the French Revolution. Nevertheless, price control measures in both ages failed entirely.

Now let us analyze the reasons for this failure. The government hears people complain that the price of milk has gone up. And milk is certainly very important, especially for the rising generation, for children. Consequently, the government declares a maximum price for milk, a maximum price that is lower than the potential market price would be. Now the government says: "Certainly we have done everything needed in order to make it possible for poor parents to buy as much milk as they need to feed their children."

But what happens? On the one hand, the lower price of milk increases the demand for milk; people who could not afford to buy milk at a higher price are now able to buy it at the lower price which the government has decreed. And on the other hand some of the producers, those producers of milk who are producing at the highest cost—that is, the marginal producers—are now suffering losses, because the price which the government has decreed is lower than their costs. This is the important point in the market economy. The private entrepreneur, the private producer, cannot take losses in the long run. And as he cannot take losses in milk, he restricts the production of milk for the market. He may sell some of his cows for the slaughter house, or instead of milk he may sell some products made out of milk, for instance sour cream, butter or cheese.

Thus the government's interference with the price of milk will result in less milk than there was before, and at the same time there will be a greater demand. Some people who are prepared to pay the government-decreed price cannot buy it. Another result will be that anxious people will hurry to be first at the shops. They have to wait outside. The long lines of people waiting at shops always appear as a familiar phenomenon in a city in which the government has decreed maximum prices for commodities that the government considers as important. This has happened everywhere when the price of milk was controlled. This was always prognosticated by economists. Of course, only by sound economists, and their number is not very great.

But what is the result of the government's price control? The government is disappointed. It wanted to increase the satisfaction of the milk drinkers. But actually it has dissatisfied them. Before the government interfered, milk was expensive, but people could buy it. Now there is only an insufficient quantity of milk available. Therefore, the total consumption of milk drops. The children are getting less milk, not more. The next measure to which the government now resorts, is rationing. But rationing only means that certain people are privileged and are getting milk while other people are *not* getting any at all. Who gets milk and who does not, of course, is always very arbitrarily determined. One order may determine, for example, that children under four years old should get milk, and that children over four years, or between the age of four and six should get only half the ration which children under four years receive.

Whatever the government does, the fact remains, there is only a smaller amount of milk available. Thus people are still more dissatisfied than they were before. Now the government asks the milk producers (because the government does not have enough imagination to find out for itself): "Why do you not produce the same amount of milk you produced before?" The government gets the answer: "We cannot do it, since the costs of production are higher than the maximum price which the government has established." Now the government studies the costs of the various items of production, and it discovers one of the items is fodder.

"Oh," says the government, "the same control we applied to milk we will now apply to fodder. We will determine a maximum price for fodder, and then you will be able to feed your cows at a lower price, at a lower expenditure. Then everything will be all right; you will be able to produce more milk and you will sell more milk."

But what happens now? The same story repeats itself with fodder, and as you can understand, for the same reasons. The production of fodder drops and the government is again faced with a dilemma. So the government arranges new hearings, to find out what is wrong with fodder production. And it gets an explanation from the producers of fodder precisely like the one it got from the milk producers. So the government must go a step farther, since it does not want to abandon the principle of price control. It determines maximum prices for producers' goods which are necessary for the production of fodder. And the same story happens again.

The government at the same time starts controlling not only milk, but also eggs, meat, and other necessities. And every time the government gets the same result, everywhere the consequence is the same. Once the government fixes a maximum price for consumer goods, it has to go farther back to producers' goods, and limit the prices of the producers' goods required for the production of the price-controlled consumer goods. And so the government, having started with only a few price controls, goes farther and farther back in the process of production, fixing maximum prices for all kinds of producers' goods, including of course the price of labor, because without wage control, the government's "cost control" would be meaningless.

Moreover, the government cannot limit its interference into the market to only those things which it views as vital necessities, like milk, butter, eggs, and meat. It must necessarily include luxury goods, because if it did not limit *their* prices, capital and labor would abandon the production of vital necessities and would turn to producing those things which the government considers unnecessary luxury goods. Thus, the isolated interference with one or a few prices of consumer goods always brings about effects—and this is important to realize—which are even *less* satisfactory than the conditions that prevailed before.

Before the government interfered, milk and eggs were expensive; after the government interfered they began to disappear from the market. The government considered those items to be so important that it interfered; it wanted to increase the quantity and improve the supply. The result was the opposite: the isolated interference brought about a condition which—from the point of view of the government—is even *more* undesirable than the previous state of affairs which the government wanted to alter. And as the government goes farther and farther, it will finally arrive at a point where all prices, all wage rates, all interest rates, in short everything in the whole economic system, is determined by the government. And this, clearly, is *socialism*.

What I have told you here, this schematic and theoretical explanation, is precisely what happened in those countries which tried to enforce a maximum price control, where governments were stubborn enough to go step by step until they came to the end. This happened in the First World War in Germany and England.

Let us analyze the situation in both countries. Both countries experienced inflation. Prices went up, and the two governments imposed price controls. Starting with a few prices, starting with only milk and eggs, they had to go farther and farther. The longer the war went on, the more inflation was generated. And after three years of war, the Germans—systematically as always—elaborated a great plan. They called it the *Hindenburg Plan*: everything in Germany considered to be good by the government at that time was named after Hindenburg.

The Hindenburg Plan meant that the whole German economic system should be controlled by the government: prices, wages, profits... everything. And the bureaucracy immediately began to put this into effect. But before they had finished, the debacle came: the German empire broke down, the entire bureaucratic apparatus disappeared, the revolution brought its bloody results—things came to an end.

In England they started in the same way, but after a time, in the spring of 1917, the United States entered the war and supplied the British with sufficient quantities of everything. Therefore the road to socialism, the road to serfdom, was interrupted.

Before Hitler came to power, Chancellor Brüning again introduced price control in Germany for the usual reasons. Hitler enforced it, even before the war started. For in Hitler's Germany there was no private enterprise or private initiative. In Hitler's Germany there was a system of socialism which differed from the Russian system only to the extent that the *terminology* and *labels* of the free economic system were still retained. There still existed "private enterprises," as they were called. But the owner was no longer an entrepreneur, the owner was called a "shop manager" (Betriebsführer).

The whole of Germany was organized in a hierarchy of führers; there was the Highest Führer, Hitler of course, and then there were führers down to the many hierarchies of smaller führers. And the head of an enterprise was the *Betriebsführer*. And the workers of the enterprise were named by a word that, in the Middle Ages, had signified the retinue of a feudal lord: the *Gefolgschaft*. And all of these people had to obey the orders issued by an institution which had a terribly long name: *Reichsführerwirtschaftsministerium*,* at the head of which was the well-known fat man, named Goering, adorned with jewelry and medals.

And from this body of ministers with the long name came all the orders to every enterprise: what to produce, in what quantity, where to get the raw materials and what to pay for them, to whom to sell the products and at what prices to sell them. The workers got the order to work in a definite factory, and they received wages which the government decreed. The whole economic system was now regulated in every detail by the government.

---

*Führer of the Reich's, i.e., the empire's Ministry of Economics

The *Betriebsführer* did not have the right to take the profits for himself; he received what amounted to a salary, and if he wanted to get more he would, for example, say: "I am very sick, I need an operation immediately, and the operation will cost 500 Marks," then he had to ask the führer of the district (the *Gauführer* or *Gauleiter*) whether he had the right to take out more than the salary which was given to him. The prices were no longer prices, the wages were no longer wages, they were all quantitative *terms* in a system of socialism.

Now let me tell you how that system broke down. One day, after years of fighting, the foreign armies arrived in Germany. They tried to preserve this government-directed economic system, but the brutality of Hitler would have been necessary to preserve it and, without this, it did not work.

And while this was going on in Germany, Great Britain—during the Second World War—did precisely what Germany did. Starting with the price control of some commodities only, the British government began step by step (in the same way Hitler had done in peacetime, even before the start of the war) to control more and more of the economy until, by the time the war ended, they had reached something that was almost pure socialism.

Great Britain was not brought to socialism by the Labour government which was established in 1945. Great Britain became socialist *during* the war, through the government of which Sir Winston Churchill was the prime minister. The Labour government simply retained the system of socialism which the government of Sir Winston Churchill had already introduced. And this in spite of great resistance by the people.

The nationalizations in Great Britain did not mean very much; the nationalization of the Bank of England was merely nominal, because the Bank of England was already under the complete control of the government. And it was the same with the nationalization of the railroads and the steel industry. The "war socialism," as it was called—meaning the system of interventionism proceeding step by step—had already virtually nationalized the system.

The difference between the German and British systems was not important since the people who operated them had been appointed by the government and in both cases they had to obey the government's orders in every respect. As I said before, the system of the German

Nazis retained the labels and terms of the capitalistic free market economy. But they meant something very different: there were now only government decrees.

This was also true for the British system. When the Conservative party in Britain was returned to power, some of those controls were removed. In Great Britain we now have attempts from one side to retain controls and from the other side to abolish them. (But one must not forget that, in England, conditions are very different from conditions in Russia.) The same is true for other countries which depend on the importation of food and raw materials and therefore have to export manufactured goods. For countries depending heavily on export trade, a system of government control simply does not work.

Thus, as far as there is economic freedom left (and there is still substantial freedom in some countries, such as Norway, England, Sweden), it exists because of the *necessity to retain export trade*. Earlier, I chose the example of milk, not because I have a special preference for milk, but because practically all governments—or most of them—in recent decades, have regulated milk, egg or butter prices.

I want to refer, in a few words, to another example, and that is rent control. If the government controls rents, one result is that people who would otherwise have moved from bigger apartments to smaller ones when their family conditions changed, will no longer do so. For example, consider parents whose children left home when they came into their twenties, married or went into other cities to work. Such parents used to change their apartments and take smaller and cheaper ones. This necessity disappeared when rent controls were imposed.

In Vienna, Austria, in the early twenties, where rent control was well-established, the amount of money that the landlord received for an average apartment under rent control was not more than twice the price of a ticket for a ride on the city-owned street cars. You can imagine that people did not have any incentive to change their apartments. And, on the other hand, there was no construction of new houses. Similar conditions prevailed in the United States after the Second World War and are continuing in many cities to this day.

One of the main reasons why many cities in the United States are in such great financial difficulty is that they have rent control and a resulting shortage of housing. So the government has spent billions for the building of new houses. But why was there such a housing shortage? The housing shortage developed for the same reasons that brought milk shortages when there was milk price control. That means: *when the government interferes with the market, it is more and more driven towards socialism.*

And this is the answer to those people who say: "We are not socialists, we do not want the government to control everything. We realize this is bad. But why should not the government interfere a little bit with the market? Why shouldn't the government do away with some things which we do not like?"

These people talk of a "middle-of-the-road" policy. What they do not see is that the *isolated* interference, which means the interference with only one small part of the economic system, brings about a situation which the government itself—and the people who are asking for government interference—find worse than the conditions they wanted to abolish: the people who are asking for rent control are very angry when they discover there is a shortage of apartments and a shortage of housing.

But this shortage of housing was created precisely by government interference, by the establishment of rents below the level people would have had to pay in a free market.

The idea that there is a *third* system—between socialism and capitalism, as its supporters say—a system as far away from socialism as it is from capitalism but that retains the advantages and avoids the disadvantages of each—is pure nonsense. People who believe there is such a mythical system can become really poetic when they praise the glories of interventionism. One can only say they are mistaken. The government interference which they praise brings about conditions which they themselves do not like.

One of the problems I will deal with later is *protectionism*. The government tries to isolate the domestic market from the world market. It introduces tariffs which raise the domestic price of a commodity above the world market price, making it possible for domestic producers to form cartels. The cartels are then attacked by the government declaring: "Under these conditions, anti-cartel legislation is necessary."

This is precisely the situation with most of the European governments. In the United States, there are yet other reasons for antitrust legislation and the government's campaign against the specter of monopoly.

It is absurd to see the government—which creates by its own intervention the conditions making possible the emergence of domestic cartels—point its finger at business, saying: "There are cartels, therefore government interference with business is necessary." It would be much simpler to avoid cartels by ending the government's interference with the market—an interference which makes these cartels possible.

The idea of government interference as a "solution" to economic problems leads, in every country, to conditions which, at the least, are very unsatisfactory and often quite chaotic. If the government does not stop in time, it will bring on socialism.

Nevertheless, government interference with business is still very popular. As soon as someone does not like something that happens in the world, he says: "The government ought to do something about it. What do we have a government for? The government should do it." And this is a characteristic remnant of thought from past ages, of ages *preceding* modern freedom, modern constitutional government, before representative government or modern republicanism.

For centuries there was the doctrine—maintained and accepted by everyone—that a king, an anointed king, was the messenger of God; he had more wisdom than his subjects, and he had supernatural powers. As recently as the beginning of the nineteenth century, people suffering from certain diseases expected to be cured by the royal touch, by the hand of the king. Doctors were usually better; nevertheless, they had their patients try the king.

This doctrine of the superiority of a paternal government, of the supernatural and superhuman powers of the hereditary kings gradually disappeared—or at least we thought so. But it came back again. There was a German professor named Werner Sombart (I knew him very well), who was known the world over, who was an honorary doctor of many universities and an honorary member of the American Economic Association. That professor wrote a book, which is available in an English translation, published by the Princeton University Press. It is available also in a French translation, and probably also in Spanish—at least I hope it is available, because then you can check what I am saying. In this book, published in our century, not in the Dark Ages,

Werner Sombart, a professor of economics, simply says: "The Führer, our Führer"—he means, of course, Hitler—"gets his orders directly from God, the Führer of the Universe."

I spoke of this hierarchy of the führers earlier, and in this hierarchy. I mentioned Hitler as the "Supreme Führer".... But there is, according to Werner Sombart, a still higher Führer, God, the Führer of the universe. And God, he wrote, gives His orders directly to Hitler. Of course, Professor Sombart said very modestly: "We do not know how God communicates with the Führer. But the fact cannot be denied."

Now, if you hear that such a book can be published in the German language, the language of a nation which was once hailed as "the nation of philosophers and poets," and if you see it translated into English and French, then you will not be astonished at the fact that even a little bureaucrat considers himself wiser and better than the citizens and wants to interfere with everything, even though he is only a poor little bureaucrat, and not the famous Professor Werner Sombart, honorary member of everything.

Is there a remedy against such happenings? I would say, yes, there is a remedy. And this remedy is the power of the citizens; they have to prevent the establishment of such an autocratic regime that arrogates to itself a higher wisdom than that of the average citizen. This is the fundamental difference between freedom and serfdom.

The socialist nations have arrogated to themselves the term *democracy*. The Russians call their own system a People's Democracy; they probably maintain that the people are represented in the person of the dictator. I think that *one* dictator, Juan Perón here in Argentina, was given a good answer when he was forced into exile in 1955. Let us hope that all other dictators, in other nations, will be accorded a similar response.

LUDWIG VON MISES

EXCERPTS FROM

THE ANTICAPITALISTIC MENTALITY

II. The Ordinary Man's Social Philosophy

1. Capitalism As It Is and As It Is Seen by the Common Man

The emergence of economics as a new branch of knowledge was one of the most portentous events in the history of mankind. In paving the way for private capitalistic enterprise it transformed within a few generations all human affairs more radically than the preceding ten thousand years had done. From the day of their birth to the day of their demise, the denizens of a capitalistic country are every minute benefited by the marvelous achievements of the capitalistic ways of thinking and acting.

The most amazing thing concerning the unprecedented change in earthly conditions brought about by capitalism is the fact that it was accomplished by a small number of authors and a hardly greater number of statesmen who had assimilated their teachings. Not only the sluggish masses but also most of the businessmen who, by their trading, made the laissez-faire principles effective failed to comprehend the essential features of their operation. Even in the heyday of liberalism only a few people had a full grasp of the functioning of the market economy. Western civilization adopted capitalism upon recommendation on the part of a small élite.

Reprinted with permission from Ludwig von Mises, *The Anticapitalistic Mentality* (Grove City, PA: Libertarian Press, 1994), pp. 27–34, 34–37. www.libertarianpress.com

There were, in the first decades of the nineteenth century, many people who viewed their own unfamiliarity with the problems concerned as a serious shortcoming and were anxious to redress it. In the years between Waterloo and Sebastopol, no other books were more eagerly absorbed in Great Britain than treatises on economics. But the vogue soon subsided. The subject was unpalatable to the general reader.

Economics is so different from the natural sciences and technology on the one hand, and history and jurisprudence on the other hand, that it seems strange and repulsive to the beginner. Its heuristic singularity is viewed with suspicion by those whose research work is performed in laboratories or in archives and libraries. Its epistemological singularity appears nonsensical to the narrow-minded fanatics of positivism. People would like to find in an economics book knowledge that perfectly fits into their preconceived image of what economics ought to be, viz., a discipline shaped according to the logical structure of physics or of biology. They are bewildered and desist from seriously grappling with problems the analysis of which requires an unwonted mental exertion.

The result of this ignorance is that people ascribe all improvements in economic conditions to the progress of the natural sciences and technology. As they see it, there prevails in the course of human history a self-acting tendency toward progressing advancement of the experimental natural sciences and their application to the solution of technological problems. This tendency is irresistible, it is inherent in the destiny of mankind, and its operation takes effect whatever the political and economic organization of society may be. As they see it, the unprecedented technological improvements of the last two hundred years were not caused or furthered by the economic policies of the age. They were not an achievement of classical liberalism, free trade, laissez faire and capitalism. They will therefore go on under any other system of society's economic organization.

The doctrines of Marx received approval simply because they adopted this popular interpretation of events and clothed it with a pseudophilosophical veil that made it gratifying both to Hegelian spiritualism and to crude materialism. In the scheme of Marx the "material productive forces" are a superhuman entity independent of the will and the actions of men. They go their own way that is prescribed by the inscrutable and inevitable laws of a higher power. They change mysteriously and force mankind to adjust its social organization to these changes; for the material productive forces shun one thing: to be enchained by mankind's social organization. The essential content of history is the struggle of the material productive forces to be freed from the social bonds by which they are fettered.

Once upon a time, teaches Marx, the material productive forces were embodied in the shape of the hand mill, and then they arranged human affairs according to the pattern of feudalism. When, later, the unfathomable laws that determine the evolution of the material productive forces substituted the steam mill for the hand mill, feudalism had to give way to capitalism. Since then the material productive forces have developed further, and their present shape imperatively requires the substitution of socialism for capitalism. Those who try to check the socialist revolution are committed to a hopeless task. It is impossible to stem the tide of historical progress.

The ideas of the so-called leftist parties differ from one another in many ways. But they agree in one point. They all look upon progressing material improvement as upon a self-acting process. The American union member takes his standard of living for granted. Fate has determined that he should enjoy amenities which were denied even to the most prosperous people of earlier generations and are still denied to many non-Americans. It does not occur to him that the "rugged individualism" of big business may have played some role in the emergence of what he calls the "American way of life." In his eyes "management" represents the unfair claims of the "exploiters" who are intent upon depriving him of his birthright. There is, he thinks, in the course of historical evolution an irrepressible tendency toward a continuous increase in the "productivity" of his labor. It is obvious that the fruits of this betterment by rights belong exclusively to him. It is his merit that—in the age of capitalism—the quotient of the value of the products turned out by the processing industries divided by the number of hands employed tended toward an increase.

The truth is that the increase in what is called the productivity of labor is due to the employment of better tools and machines. A hundred workers in a modern factory produce per unit of time a multiple of what a hundred workers used to produce in the workshops of pre-capitalistic craftsmen. This improvement is not conditioned by higher skill, competence or application on the part of the individual worker. (It is a fact that the proficiency needed by medieval artisans towered far above that of many categories of present-day factory hands.) It is due to the employment of more efficient tools and machines which, in turn, is the effect of the accumulation and investment of more capital.

The terms capitalism, capital, and capitalists were employed by Marx and are today employed by most people—also by the official propaganda agencies of the United States government—with an opprobrious connotation. Yet these words pertinently point toward the main factor whose operation produced all the marvelous achieve-ments of the last two hundred years: the unprecedented improve-ment of the average standard of living for a continually increasing population. What distinguishes modern industrial conditions in the capitalistic countries from those of the precapitalistic ages as well as from those prevailing today in the so-called underdeveloped countries is the amount of the supply of capital. No technological improvement can be put to work if the capital required has not previously been ac-cumulated by saving.

Saving—capital accumulation—is the agency that has trans-formed step by step the awkward search for food on the part of savage cave dwellers into the modern ways of industry. The pacemakers of this evolution were the ideas that created the institutional framework within which capital accumulation was rendered safe by the principle of private ownership of the means of production. Every step forward on the way toward prosperity is the effect of saving. The most in-genious technological inventions would be practically useless if the capital goods required for their utilization had not been accumulated by saving.

The entrepreneurs employ the capital goods made available by the savers for the most economical satisfaction of the most urgent among the not-yet-satisfied wants of the consumers. Together with the technologists, intent upon perfecting the methods of processing, they play, next to the savers themselves, an active part in the course of events that is called economic progress. The rest of mankind profit from the activities of these three classes of pioneers. But whatever their own doings may be, they are only beneficiaries of changes to the emergence of which they did not contribute anything.

The characteristic feature of the market economy is the fact that it allots the greater part of the improvements brought about by the endeavors of the three progressive classes—those saving, those investing the capital goods, and those elaborating new methods for the employment of capital goods to the nonprogressive majority of people. Capital accumulation exceeding the increase in population raises, on the one hand, the marginal productivity of labor and, on the other hand, cheapens the products. The market process provides the common man with the opportunity to enjoy the fruits of other peoples' achievements. It forces the three progressive classes to serve the nonprogressive majority in the best possible way.

Everybody is free to join the ranks of the three progressive classes of a capitalist society. These classes are not closed castes. Membership in them is not a privilege conferred on the individual by a higher authority or inherited from one's ancestors. These classes are not clubs, and the "ins" have no power to keep out any newcomer. What is needed to become a capitalist, an entrepreneur, or a deviser of new technological methods is brains and will power. The heir of a wealthy man enjoys a certain advantage as he starts under more favorable conditions than others. But his task in the rivalry of the market is not easier, but sometimes even more wearisome and less remunerative than that of a newcomer. He has to reorganize his inheritance in order to adjust it to the changes in market conditions. Thus, for instance, the problems that the heir of a railroad "empire" had to face were, in the last decades, certainly knottier than those encountered by the man who started from scratch in trucking or in air transportation.

The popular philosophy of the common man misrepresents all these facts in the most lamentable way. As John Doe sees it, all those new industries that are supplying him with amenities unknown to his father came into being by some mythical agency called progress. Capital accumulation, entrepreneurship and technological ingenuity did not contribute anything to the spontaneous generation of prosperity. If any man has to be credited with what John Doe considers as the rise in the productivity of labor, then it is the man on the assembly line. Unfortunately, in this sinful world there is exploitation of man by man. Business skims the cream and leaves, as the Communist Manifesto points out, to the creator of all good things, to the manual worker, not more than "he requires for his maintenance and for the propagation of his race." Consequently, "the modern worker, instead of rising with the progress of industry, sinks deeper and deeper.... He becomes a pauper, and pauperism develops more rapidly than population and wealth." The authors of this description of capitalistic industry are praised at universities as the greatest philosophers and benefactors of mankind and their teachings are accepted with reverential awe by the millions whose homes, besides other gadgets, are equipped with radio and television sets.

The worst exploitation, say professors, "labor" leaders, and politicians is effected by big business. They fail to realize that the characteristic mark of big business is mass production for the satisfaction of the needs of the masses. Under capitalism the workers themselves, directly or indirectly, are the main consumers of all those things that the factories are turning out.

In the early days of capitalism there was still a considerable time lag between the emergence of an innovation and its becoming accessible to the masses. About sixty years ago Gabriel Tarde was right in pointing out that an industrial innovation is the fancy of a minority before it becomes the need of everybody; what was considered first as an extravagance turns later into a customary requisite of all and sundry. This statement was still correct with regard to the popularization of the automobile. But big-scale production by big business has shortened and almost eliminated this time lag. Modern innovations can only be produced profitably according to the methods of mass production and hence become accessible to the many at the very moment of their practical inauguration. There was, for instance, in the United States no sensible period in which the enjoyment of such innovations as television, nylon stockings or canned baby food was reserved to a minority of the well-to-do. Big business tends, in fact, toward a standardization of the peoples' ways of consumption and enjoyment.

Nobody is needy in the market economy because of the fact that some people are rich. The riches of the rich are not the cause of the poverty of anybody. The process that makes some people rich is, on the contrary, the corollary of the process that improves many peoples' want satisfaction. The entrepreneurs, the capitalists and the technologies prosper as far as they succeed in best supplying the consumers.

2. The Anticapitalistic Front

From the very beginnings of the socialist movement and the endeavors to revive the interventionist policies of the precapitalistic ages, both socialism and interventionism were utterly discredited in the eyes of those conversant with economic theory. But the ideas of the immense majority of ignorant people exclusively driven by the most powerful human passions of envy and hatred.

The social philosophy of the Enlightenment that paved the way for the realization of the liberal program—economic freedom, consummated in the market economy (capitalism), and its constitutional corallary, representative government—did not suggest the annihilation of the three old powers: the monarchy, the aristocracy and the churches. The European liberals aimed at the substitution of the parliamentary monarchy for royal absolutism, not at the establishment of republican government. They wanted to abolish the privileges of the aristocrats, but not to deprive them of their titles, their escutcheons, and their estates. They were eager to grant to everybody freedom of conscience and to put an end to the persecution of dissenters and heretics, but they were anxious to give to all churches and denominations perfect freedom in the pursuit of their spiritual objectives. Thus the three great powers of the *ancien régime* were preserved. One might have expected that princes, aristocrats and clergymen who indefatigably professed their conservatism would be prepared to oppose the socialist attack upon the essentials of Western civilization. After all, the harbingers of socialism did not shrink from disclosing that under socialist totalitarianism no room would be left for what they called the remnants of tyranny, privilege, and superstition.

However, even with these privileged groups resentment and envy were more intense than cool reasoning. They virtually joined hands with the socialists disregarding the fact that socialism aimed also at the confiscation of their holdings and that there cannot be any religious freedom under a totalitarian system. The Hohenzollern in Germany inaugurated a policy that an American observer called monarchical socialism.* The autocratic Romanovs of Russia toyed with labor unionism as a weapon to fight the "bourgeois" endeavors to establish representative government.** In every European country the aristo-crats were virtually cooperating with the enemies of capitalism. Everywhere eminent theologians tried to discredit the free enterprise system and thus, by implication, to support either socialism or radical interventionism. Some of the outstanding leaders of present-day Protestantism—Barth and Brunner in Switzerland, Niebuhr and Tillich in the United States, and the late Archbishop of Canterbury, William Temple—openly condemn capitalism and even charge the alleged failures of capitalism with the responsibility for all the excesses of Russian Bolshevism.

One may wonder whether Sir William Harcourt was right when, more than sixty years ago, he proclaimed: We are all socialists now. But today governments, political parties, teachers and writers, militant antitheists as well as Christian theologians are almost unanimous in passionately rejecting the market economy and praising the alleged benefits of state omnipotence. The rising generation is brought up in an environment that is engrossed in socialist ideas.

The influence of the prosocialist ideology comes to light in the way in which public opinion, almost without any exception, explains the reasons that induce people to join the socialist or communist parties. In dealing with domestic politics, one assumes that, "naturally and necessarily," those who are not rich favor the radical programs—planning, socialism, communism—while only the rich have reason to vote for the preservation of the market economy. This assumption takes for granted the fundamental socialist idea that the economic interests of the masses are hurt by the operation of capitalism for the sole benefit of the "exploiters" and that socialism will improve the common man's standard of living.

---

*Cf. Elmer Roberts, *Monarchical Socialism in Germany*, New York, 1913.
**Cf. Mania Gordon, *Workers Before and After Lenin*, New York, 1941, pp. 30 ff.

However, people do not ask for socialism because they know that socialism will improve their conditions, and they do not reject capitalism because they know that it is a system prejudicial to their interests. They are socialists because they *believe* that socialism will improve their conditions, and they hate capitalism because they *believe* that it harms them. They are socialists because they are blinded by envy and ignorance. They stubbornly refuse to study economics and spurn the economists' devastating critique of the socialist plans because, in their eyes, economics, being an abstract theory, is simply nonsense. They pretend to trust only in experience. But they no less stubbornly refuse to take cognizance of the undeniable facts of experience, viz., that the common man's standard of living is incomparably higher in capitalistic America than in the socialist paradise of the Soviets.

In dealing with conditions in the economically backward countries people display the same faulty reasoning. They think that these peoples must "naturally" sympathize with communism because they are poverty-stricken. Now it is obvious that the poor nations want to get rid of their penury. Aiming at an improvement of their unsatisfactory conditions, they ought therefore to adopt that system of society's economic organization which best warrants the attainment of this end; they ought to decide in favor of capitalism. But, deluded by spurious anticapitalistic ideas, they are favorably disposed to communism. It is paradoxical indeed that the leaders of these Oriental peoples, while casting longing glances at the prosperity of the Western nations, reject the methods that made the West prosperous and are enraptured by Russian communism that is instrumental in keeping the Russians and their satellites poor. It is still more paradoxical that Americans, enjoying the products of capitalistic big business, exalt the Soviet system and consider it quite "natural" that the poor nations of Asia and Africa should prefer communism to capitalism.

People may disagree on the question of whether everybody ought to study economics seriously. But one thing is certain. A man who publicly talks or writes about the opposition between capitalism and socialism without having fully familiarized himself with all that economics has to say about these issues is an irresponsible babbler.